Persecuted and Forgotten?

A Report on Christians oppressed for their Faith

2011 Edition

Aid to the Church in Need

Persecuted and Forgotten?
A Report on Christians oppressed for their Faith – 2011 Edition
© 2011 **Aid to the Church in Need**. All rights reserved.

Edited by John Pontifex and John Newton

Published by
Aid to the Church in Need
12–14 Benhill Avenue
Sutton, Surrey
SM1 4DA
United Kingdom
Tel: 020 8642 8668   Email: acn@acnuk.org
Fax: 020 8661 6293   Website: www.acnuk.org

A registered charity in England & Wales (1097984) and Scotland (SC040748)

Cover image: A demonstration in Detroit, Michigan, USA, calling for increased protection for Christians in Iraq. The rally was held a week after the 31st October 2010 siege at Baghdad's Syrian Catholic Cathedral of Our Lady of Deliverance where 58 people died and more than 70 were injured. (Photo: ©AP/Paul Sancya). Cover design by John Newton.

Printed in the UK by CPI William Clowes, Beccles, NR34 7TL

ISBN 978-0-9553339-6-5

Foreword by Archbishop Fouad Twal, Latin Patriarch of Jerusalem

"If anybody wants to follow me, he must take up his cross." (Luke 14:27) These words of Jesus Christ echo down the centuries from his time to our own. In many parts of the world – not least in the Middle East – we know that carrying the cross lies at the heart of Christian life.

Calvary is not a name that belongs only to archaeology and antiquity. It is a contemporaneous reality that describes, to differing degrees, the suffering of many churches in the Middle East where to be Christian means accepting that you must make a great sacrifice. All too often and in many places, Christians suffer verbal abuse, discrimination in the workplace, taunts in the media and various threats. On some occasions, their homes and churches are burnt, and people – themselves, their loved ones and neighbours, even their priests and bishops – are killed. Those who live in the shadow of violence and intolerance may struggle to understand the meaning of their suffering. Weeping and crying, they often ask themselves: "Does anybody hear our cry? How many atrocities must we endure before somebody somewhere comes to our aid?"

Being a Christian in those lands is no accident of birth. It is part of our vocation. We need to go deeper into our experience and realise that our pain and misery unites us to Christ.

3

Many Christians have left the Middle East. Perhaps it was for economic reasons, perhaps due to the lack of a secure environment, or because religious extremism is on the rise. When Christians are bruised and battered by those who assail them, they are similar to Christ who also fell to the ground under the weight of the Cross.

It is a travesty of justice to turn a blind eye, as so many do. Yet, in truth, it is hard to motivate people to respond unless they know the story of people in these situations. *Persecuted and Forgotten? A Report on Christians oppressed for their Faith* sets out to faithfully record the details of the suffering they endure – not just in the Middle East, but in so many other countries where the faithful suffer. This book bears witness to the courage, the commitment and the Christ-like example of so many people – young and old alike – who carry their cross today. If they still have hope against all odds, it is because of their faith in Christ and because of the many people of good will who endeavour to stand by them. God's grace inspires many friends and benefactors to amazing acts of prayer, compassion and generosity.

We trust in God. We do not forget the promise Christ made while he was with us: "I give you peace, peace that the world cannot give."

I would personally like to thank the authors of this courageous book. I extend my gratitude to Aid to the Church in Need – which I have known for many years – for publishing it and for their compassionate aid to suffering Christians in many countries. They embody the Lord's compassion and paternal love.

+ Fouad Twal, Latin Patriarch of Jerusalem

Contents

Introduction 6
Afghanistan.. 12
Algeria.. 14
Bangladesh 16
Belarus... 19
Bosnia–Herzegovina 21
Burma (Myanmar) 23
China 25
Cuba 32
Democratic Republic of the Congo 35
Egypt 37
Profile: Bishop Kyrillos William of Assiut, Egypt.................................... 42
Eritrea 45
India... 50
Profile: Sister Meena from Orissa, India 56
Indonesia... 59
Iran.. 62
Iraq.. 66
Profile: Archbishop Amil Nona of Mosul, Iraq 72
Israel and Palestine 75
Kazakhstan 80
Laos 84
Lebanon... 86
Maldives.. 89
Nigeria 91
North Korea 94
Pakistan 96
Profile: Almas Hameed from Gojra, Pakistan....................................... 103
Philippines 105
Russia 107
Saudi Arabia.. 110
Sri Lanka.. 113
Sudan 119
Profile: Bishop Akio Johnson of Torit, Sudan 123
Turkey.. 125
Venezuela 127
Vietnam.. 130
Yemen.. 136

Introduction

"We are easy targets. I fear for my brothers and sisters in the Christian faith. Again and again, our people are hurt and killed, our churches are damaged and destroyed. The faithful feel they have no option but to leave. Politicians at home and abroad may sympathise with us but in the final analysis the Christian people see no end to their suffering and so they keep asking us: 'Who can we turn to?' "

As he spoke, it was clear that Archbishop Bashar Warda felt there was no point concealing the extent of the problems facing Christians in Iraq. Monsignor Warda was barely 40 when his nomination as a bishop in Iraq was announced in early 2010. As such, according to Church sources, he became the world's youngest diocesan Catholic bishop.[1] But if the opening months were anything to go by, life as Archbishop of Erbil was enough to test his youth and optimism to breaking point. And the toughest test yet was not long in coming. Barely two weeks after our conversation in Rome came the siege of Our Lady of Deliverance Syrian Catholic Cathedral in Baghdad. In that crime of unprecedented severity, which took place during Sunday Mass on 31st October 2010, 58 people were killed and more than 70 were injured. Reflecting on my conversation with the young archbishop in the weeks and months that followed, neither of us realised how true and prophetic were the words he uttered.

The Synod of Bishops of the Middle East, held in Rome where I met the archbishop, took place amid growing concern about the future of Christianity in the land of Christ. The ever-deepening catastrophe unfolding in this, the Cradle of Christianity, is far deeper than many media reports suggest. And that provides a key *raison d'être* behind this, Aid to the Church in Need's 2011 edition of *Persecuted and Forgotten? A Report on Christians oppressed for their Faith.*

Not that the Middle East is the publication's sole preoccupation. The third edition of a series that first appeared in the autumn of 2006, *Persecuted and Forgotten? 2011* expands the range of countries under consideration. A total of 33 countries are covered in the book – from Afghanistan right through to Yemen. More countries have been included in the report to reflect the increasing and widening problems Christians have been facing. Having said that, some countries have been included less because of the suffering endured by Christians there and more because they are of key importance politically and in terms of ecumenical or inter-faith relations at the highest level. Russia is a notable example of this. The report draws on world-wide research carried out by journalists and other investigating teams, who helped prepare ACN's recent *Religious Freedom Report* examining the situation in almost every country concerning all faith communities. Because *Persecuted and Forgotten?* is focused on Christian persecution, extra research has been undertaken, drawing on reports by human rights organisations, major news providers and most importantly ACN's own close contacts through the charity's project partners, the bishops and other senior Catholic figures.

Persecuted and Forgotten? is specifically concerned with violent acts perpetrated against Christians – be they Catholic, Orthodox or Protestant. To qualify for inclusion in the report, there must be evidence that the violent act in question is at least partly motivated by religious intolerance. For example, the murder of a catechist in Sudan, however shocking, is not in itself enough to warrant an entry in the book. It may be that it is a case of mistaken identity or a mugging that went horribly wrong. But sadly, as becomes clear in so many of the book's country reports, bishops, priests, Sisters and lay people have sometimes paid the ultimate price as the victims of religious bigotry and indeed hatred. Each country report is headed with an introduction drawing out the major themes concerning human rights for Christians, looking at political, social and of course religious developments over the past two years and more. As well as highlighting many of the key facts and figures, each country report then proceeds to look behind the statistics to reveal some of the men, women and children caught up in a climate of hostility. In the incident log that follows each country's introduction, the report details some of the most significant incidents of violence and intimidation over the period in question. Some of the reports make for unavoidably distressing reading and hence the book may be judged inappropriate for very young children and other vulnerable people.

This we believe is a risk worth running. The report's overarching objective is to raise awareness of the cold-blooded brutality that frequently characterises man's inhumanity to man. And no more so it seems than when the man (or woman) under attack happens to be a Christian. As Aid to the Church in Need can testify, thanks to its work in 140 project countries, what most distresses the bishops, priests, Sisters and lay people

7

we know so well is that the West is seemingly indifferent to the suffering of the faithful. One prelate whose faithful suffer severe violence spoke out recently against the luke-warm international response to the people's plight, saying it was directly linked to the failure of the authorities to provide adequate protection. He said: "Let us break the wall of silence that surrounds the killing of Christians. Christians are killed while the state does nothing. The forces of order serving in the places of the attacks and killings don't see, don't hear, don't speak."

This failure to acknowledge the crimes against Christianity could not be more tragic, coming at a time when in key countries the violence and intimidation of the faithful have manifestly worsened. And this is noticeable even compared with the situation of three years ago, covered in the 2008 *Persecuted and Forgotten?*. Of the countries where Christians are suffering more than before, the most notable examples are first and foremost Iraq but also elsewhere in the Middle East and wider Muslim world including Egypt, Lebanon, Pakistan and Turkey. At the time we went to press, Sudan was at risk of widespread violence.

The rise of extremist Islam is well documented as a worldwide phenomenon. The sheer number and variety of attacks show that all groups – including many Muslims – are potential targets. What seems to have changed however is that Christians in Muslim countries are now especially vulnerable and those responsible for crimes against them are quite open about their contempt for the Church. By 2011, organisations promoting human rights for Christians were noting the increased threat posed by Islamism, especially extremist movements originating in Saudi Arabia.[2] The long-standing justification for Islamist attacks against Christians is related to heightened sensitivity concerning Christian proselytism and allegations of disrespect shown to the *Qur'an* and the Prophet Mohammed. Extremists increasingly link local Christians in their countries to the West. According to Islamists, leading nations – especially the USA – stand accused of being latter-day crusaders intent on supplanting Islam in its homelands. As they are in most cases unable to attack Western countries direct, many extremists turn their fire on local Christians.

There is also a new factor to consider. As witnessed in Iraq and in some other countries, the express wish of the extremists is undoubtedly to wipe out Christianity from their land. The attacks in Mosul in 2008-09 and the

October 2010 siege of the Syrian Catholic Cathedral in Baghdad are two obvious examples of this. In both cases it became apparent that extremists sought the removal of the country's Christian presence. Such fundamentalists are spurred on by the fact that what they wish to see happen is already close to coming to pass. It is no exaggeration to say that in the past 150 years an exodus of Christians on a truly Biblical scale has taken place in many parts of the Middle East. In some cases, this has happened within a generation. Iraq, however, is by far the most serious. At the time of the last census in 1987 the country was home to 1.4 million Christians. By the beginning of 2003, that figure had fallen to 800,000. By the beginning of 2011, the media was giving 500,000 as the country's Christian population but leading Catholic prelates in Iraq have told Aid to the Church in Need that the real figure could be as low as 150,000. Of those still in Iraq, many – if not most – were living as displaced people desperate to join family and friends in neighbouring Jordan and Syria before travelling to the West.

So many countries in the Middle East have their own story to tell of the decline of Christianity – be it through mass exodus of faithful or much higher birth-rates among other faith communities. In 2009, Archbishop Fouad Twal dedicated his first pastoral letter as Patriarch of Jerusalem to the subject of Christian emigration, noting that since 1948 (Palestinian) Christians in Bethlehem had declined from 85 percent of the population to 12 percent. In the 2008 edition of *Persecuted and Forgotten?* the question concerning the Middle East seemed to be about the gradual decline of Christianity into obscurity. Now the question is much more painful: will future historians say of us that we were firsthand witnesses to the extinguishing of Christianity in the very countries where the light of our faith first took hold? Nor is this just a question for Christians in Muslim countries. Elsewhere in his 2009 pastoral letter, Patriarch Twal states that in Jerusalem, (Palestinian) Christians were now 1.1 percent compared with 20 percent 60 years previously. This comes at a time when Christian leaders in Israel have reported a hardening of attitudes against Christians amid signs that an intolerant hard-line Judaism is in the ascendancy.

And this points to another key theme of 2011's *Persecuted and Forgotten?*: that in non-Muslim countries too there have been manifest signs of increasing radicalisation of religious groups and a corresponding growing antipathy to Christianity. This is especially visible among Hindu extremists in India as witnessed by the 2007-08 outbreaks of persecution in the state of Orissa, violence subsequently replicated in much smaller incidents in very different parts of the country. For the extremists who damaged 6,000 homes and caused the displacement of more than 50,000 people, an attack on Christianity was an act of patriotism. Christianity was seen as inextricably linked to Western liberalism and hence was a threat to the God-given identity of the nation-state. In Burma, the military junta attacked Christians as a strategic strike against both ethnic rebels and other forces deemed to be undermining the country's staunchly Buddhist identity. Taken as a whole, a politicisation of religion has widened and deepened the problem of Christian persecution.

Nationalism of a different kind explains why oppression of Christians has grown in Latin America. The inclusion of Venezuela in this report is the result of a sudden and dramatic upsurge of anti-Catholic violence and intimidation led by governments inspired by the ideals of 'socialism' with which Fidel Castro's Cuba is most associated. This is ironic when in Cuba itself, the Catholic Church would appear to have achieved a breakthrough in relations with the state, holding out the prospect of an end to suspicion and hostility dating back half a century.

In parts of the world where persecution of Christians is largely political by nature, there are two countries of particular note. North Korea is where Christians are probably persecuted the most. Meanwhile in neighbouring China, Christians suffer violence and intimidation, their churches closed down, their bishops and priests under house-arrest. That said, elsewhere in the country and at different times, the situation seems much improved, with religious freedom afforded to a degree unthinkable a generation ago. Indeed, change for the better has been noted in a number of communist and former communist regimes notorious for their anti-Christian activities in earlier times.[3]

Taken as a whole then, is persecution of Christians getting worse? The findings of this report show that the situation is mixed. However, significant developments in key countries point to the inescapable conclusion that – especially in the Middle East and some other countries – Christianity is under threat as never before and could yet disappear. Research into the total number of Christians suffering persecution gives varying statistics but all of them are alarming. In autumn 2010, the

Commission of the Bishops' Conferences of the European Community (COMECE) reported that at least 75 percent of all religious persecution was directed at Christians. COMECE also stated that 100 million people were discriminated against or persecuted. Human rights and other organisations gave a similar figure. If it comes as a shock to discover that in some regions oppression of Christians today is as bad as it ever was, then it is all the more apt that we should have entitled this report "Persecuted and Forgotten?". What it amounts to is a human rights disaster of epic proportions and action is urgently needed at all levels. Silence and inaction are inexcusable.

The urgency of the problem was spelled out by Pope Benedict XVI in his Message for World Peace Day, 1st January 2011. In what was widely understood to be a reference to the COMECE report, the Pontiff declared that Christians are the religious group who suffer the most persecution and added: "Many Christians experience daily affronts and often live in fear because of their pursuit of truth, their faith in Christ Jesus and their heartfelt plea for respect for religious freedom. This situation is unacceptable since it represents an insult to God and to human dignity."[4]

For Aid to the Church in Need, the Catholic charity which has produced this report, the prevailing theme is clear: now more than ever, Christians need help and support. The charity is committed to keeping the light of the Christian faith burning in countries of persecution and oppression. ACN believes in the power of prayer and asks people of all faiths to join us in calling on God to relieve the sufferings of those stricken by pain and fear. For ACN, prayer is inextricably linked with action. Every year the charity fulfils about 5,000 projects in 140 countries. Child's Bibles, Mass stipends, church building and help for refugees are but some examples of the aid provided. Spurring the charity on are the individual stories we hear from priests and people determined to keep the faith no matter what. When Archbishop Bashar Warda of Iraq spoke up on behalf of his people and asked me: "Who can we turn to?", I had no hesitation in assuring him of the constant prayers and support of ACN. For as ACN's late founder Fr Werenfried van Straaten so famously said: "They are being tested in faith; we are being tested in love."

John Pontifex

Afghanistan

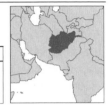

Population	Religions	Christian Population
29 million	Sunni Muslim 80% Shi'a Muslim 19% Other 1%	Less than 2,500

The dangers of being a Christian in Afghanistan were brought into sharp relief in summer 2010 when a group of former Muslims sentenced to death for converting to Christianity gave an interview after escaping to India. The group, who were not named for security reasons, appealed for protection for religious minorities. The visit coincided with increased media reports of violence and threats against Christians, possibly associated with reports of US soldiers involved in proselytism. Throughout the period under review, groups claiming responsibility for violence against Western organisations in Afghanistan tended to justify their attacks by making allegations of proselytism. Overall, human rights and religious freedom organisations noted a dramatic deterioration in attitudes towards non-Muslims.

Many Afghanistan experts trace the problems back to the country's constitution, which is criticised as ambiguous. On the one hand, the constitution makes reference to the Universal Declaration of Human Rights (Article 7), stating that religions other than Islam are "free to exercise their faith and perform their religious rites within the limits of the provisions of the law". On the other hand, Islam is declared to be the state religion. Article 3 states: "No law can be contrary to the beliefs and provisions of the sacred religion of Islam." Hence *Shari'a* is widely enforced and there are very serious punishments both for Muslims and those who convert.

Well-placed Church sources close to ACN indicate that Christians can practise their faith in the few places designated for the purpose, provided they keep a very low profile and thereby avoid accusations of proselytism. However, although Christians are very few, their presence is liable to create tension in a country proud of its staunchly Muslim identity. The influence of the Taleban, local mullahs and imams is very powerful, especially in rural areas. Human rights organisations have voiced concerns about women's rights. Overall, the prospects of an improvement in religious freedom for Christians remain bleak and if anything the situation is likely to worsen.

February 2009: Acts of violence and intimidation against Christians in Afghanistan dramatically worsened over the course of the previous year according to Open Doors, the international organisation for the rights of Christians. Its annual report showed Afghanistan rose three places to become the world's fourth-worst country for Christian persecution. It cited increased pressure from the Taleban and an increasingly hostile climate for non-Muslims.[5]

May 2010: *Noorin TV*, a local television station, broadcast a documentary showing footage and photographs of secret "Afghan Christian Converts". The programme was followed by riots and demonstrations across the country. Protestors invoked *Shari'a* law, as enshrined in the constitution, calling for the arrest of the 'culprits' and the execution of converts from Islam. Public figures also called for action, with one lawmaker stating that it was "not a crime" to kill a Muslim who converts to Christianity. Waheed Omar, spokesman for Afghan President Hamid Karai, told reporters that the president had ordered an investigation by the country's secret service.[6]

June 2010: A group of Afghans, sentenced to death for converting from Islam to Christianity, fled to India and called on the international community to take action to ensure religious rights are protected and save converts at risk of execution. The group were sentenced on 31st May, four days after *Noorin TV*'s documentary on converts to Christianity. Also in June 2010 more than 20 Christians were detained in Afghanistan after political leaders called for the arrest and execution of converts.[7]

July 2010: UK MP Tim Farron put forward an early day motion in the UK House of Commons calling on the Afghan government to safeguard the lives of converts from Islam following the upsurge of anti-Christian violence.[8]

August 2010: Christian group International Assistance Mission suffered the greatest tragedy in its 44-year history of operations in Afghanistan when 10 members of an eye care team were massacred in mountains in the north of the country. There were six Americans, one German, one Briton and two Afghans. The Taleban claimed responsibility for the attack, accusing the medical volunteers of being foreign spies and trying to convert Muslims to Christianity. The group denied the claims.[9]

Algeria

Population	Religions	Christian Population
34.5 million[10]	Sunni Muslim 99% Other 1%	30-50,000

Widespread reports of thousands of Muslims converting to Christianity have alarmed both the government and extremist groups, which are determined to retain Algeria's strongly Muslim identity. There has been an upsurge in court cases and acts of intimidation against Christian converts. The pretext for such attacks has been allegations of proselytism in direct contravention of the constitution. And yet, although Islam is the official state religion, the constitution also defends the right to freedom of thought and religious practice within defined limitations. Compounding the problem of anti-Christian sentiment is the fact that 95 percent of Christians are foreigners (Europeans, Lebanese, students from sub-Saharan Africa and Americans). Most come for work and stay for a maximum of two years. Hence Christians are seen as outsiders and are often viewed with suspicion.

During 2009-11, a big test for minority groups – especially Christians – has been the question of the enforcement of the 2006 religion law. From earliest days, the law was seen as controversial, since it clashes with Algeria's (1996) constitution, which declares that religious freedom is inviolable. Of particular concern in the 2006 law is an article stating that minority groups found guilty of evangelising among Muslims are liable to five-year prison sentences and fines of up to US$14,000 (£9,000, €10,770). The law also requires non-Islamic 'religious meetings' be held in authorised premises. For the Catholic Church, this has not represented so much of a problem because it has a number of recognised places of worship. Protestants by contrast have very few authorised churches and chapels.

In early 2008, 30 churches were forcibly closed, but by the end of 2009, at least 20 had reopened despite not obtaining the requisite registration. However, other churches were forced to close and still more were attacked. Senior Church sources close to Aid to the Church in Need said the overall situation for Christians in Algeria has worsened since 2008. They reported that extremists had stirred up ill-feeling towards their faithful and that government attitudes against Christians had hardened, with more priests, religious and lay people being refused visas and other travel permits.

July 2009: Two Christians, Rachid Mohammed Seghir, 40, and Jammal Dahmani, 36, were each given a US$1,250 (£800, €960) fine and a six-month suspended jail term after being found guilty of trying to convert Muslims. The court, in Tissemsilt, 150 miles (240 km) south-west of Algiers, heard that police investigations began during a routine check when extracts of the Bible were found in the Christians' car. They were also accused of using a building not authorised for religious services. [11]

December 2009: During a Christmas service on 26th December, 20 Muslims attacked a newly-built Protestant church used by Christian converts. During the night of 28th December, the attackers returned, burgling the building before desecrating it. Christians continued to gather in the building but another group of attackers burst in on 2nd January 2010, disrupting a service. A week later, everything was burnt – furniture, Bibles, hymnbooks and a cross.

February 2010: Archbishop Ghaleb Bader of Algiers spoke out in defence of the rights of the Church during a conference on freedom of religion held in the capital. He called for a review of the March 2006 law on religious practice. He said the government was increasingly turning down visa applications from Catholic priests and religious: "If priests and nuns are refused visas, the life of the Church will be gradually snuffed out."

August 2010: Two construction workers, Hocine Hocini, 44, and Salem Fellak, 34, both recent converts from Islam, were arrested during their lunch break. They were charged with "non-compliance with a precept of Islam" for eating during daylight hours during Ramadan. Six weeks later, the court prosecutor in Ain el-Hammam, a town in Kabylie, requested that each serve a three-year jail sentence. Hocine Hocini told the court he was a Christian. In response, the prosecutor told him "to leave this country, a land of Islam". Outside the courthouse, demonstrators in their hundreds – human rights activists, liberal Muslims, intellectuals and atheists – showed their support for the two men, singing Christian hymns and protesting about "arbitrary use of power". On 5th October, hundreds once again gathered outside the courthouse and finally heard that the two men had been acquitted. [12]

Bangladesh

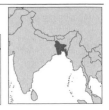

Population	Religions	Christian Population
165.5 million	Muslim 88.5% Hindu 9.5% Other 1.5% Christian 0.5%	828,000

Widespread concern about civil liberties in Bangladesh was sparked in the summer of 2009 when Dipal Barua, one of the region's most respected human rights activists, declared that "attacks against minorities are increasing at a staggering rate". Fundamentalists have been blamed for an growing number of atrocities and acts of intimidation against Christians and other minorities. Until recently, reports indicated that threats of Islamist violence towards Christians were only sparked by alleged evangelistic outreach to Muslims. Now, senior Church sources have told Aid to the Church in Need that Christians are at risk even if they confine their ministry to tribal groups who follow ancient pagan religions.

In response to threats from extremists, the government has had no choice but to concede to demands to improve security for Christians, especially at major religious festivals. The threats do not seem to have deterred the faithful from attending services. In Easter 2009, for example, as many as 300,000 people in Dhaka, the capital, attended Easter celebrations, which took place amid tight security. Police officer Abu Sayed said: "The same scenario is repeated throughout the country: people gather in churches protected by the police...We are not able to guarantee the security of people in everyday life."

Christians have also faced persecution from Buddhist extremists in the Chittagong Hills, in the three districts of Bandarban, Khagrachuri and Rangamati. These extremists, who have links to armed rebels of the United Peoples Democratic Front, have tried to stop Christians reading the Bible or praying to Jesus. Reports say that Christians are not allowed to enter Buddhist villages, buy or sell food, use bridges, ferries, or roads. The Rev Leor P Sarkar, general secretary of the Bangladesh Baptist Church Fellowship, said extremists "simply persecute them for their faith in Christ".[13]

June 2009: After discovering that his son Jahirul had converted to Christianity, Aminul Islam started beating his wife for allowing the boy to study abroad. Jahirul suggested that his mother should turn to the Rev Alex Khan for support, and in September the woman announced her own conversion to Christianity. In response, Aminul Islam burned his wife's Bible, tied up the woman and her daughter and brutally beat them. The two women reported that "they were afraid, but were comforted by their prayers."

July-August 2009: The Muslim family of Christian convert Rashidul Amin Khandaker was ostracised and their home was destroyed. Rashidul's father Ruhil was prevented from entering a mosque to pray and was threatened by extremists, who ordered him to kill his son.

August-September 2009: The Catholic community in Solepur was the object of a number of violent attacks by Muslim extremists, who tried to force them to leave so they could occupy their land.

September 2009: Mohammed Mijan Bandari, the local leader of the Bangladesh Nationalist Party, attacked Mohammed Faruk. The incident took place on 23rd September when Mohammed Faruk was on a trip to visit his cousin, William Gomes, a Catholic convert from Islam. William Gomes intervened to defend Mohammed Faruk, receiving death threats from Mohammed Bandari and a group of about 100 Islamists. When police arrived the crowd dispersed. Two days later, Mr Gomes fled his home after it was torched by Muslim militants.

September 2009: Members of the Hizbut Tawhid Islamic movement attacked 25-year-old Christian student Anup Rodrigues in Dhaka. Mr Rodrigues said four people dressed in traditional Muslim garments attacked him from behind. One of the attackers accused him of insulting the Prophet Mohammed and described Christians as "the curse of the nation" as they "want to convert Muslims". The attackers began to beat Mr Rodrigues with iron and bamboo sticks. "While they beat me I prayed to the Virgin Mary to save me. As soon as I was provided with an opportunity I ran away."

October 2009: About 150 Muslims occupied the family home of a Catholic man, Sunil Gomes. During the attack, on 8th October, they removed the house's nameplate bearing the Gomes family name and a small crucifix, replacing them with one bearing the words "Allah Akbar" (God is great).

17

On 22nd October shots were fired at the house. Subsequently, neighbours put pressure on the Catholic family to move but they were reluctant because of the advanced age and ill health of Mr Gomes's parents.

February 2010: Christian worker Edward Biswas, 32, was beaten by about 20 people in Chandpur village, Feni district, about 93 miles (150 km) south-east of Dhaka. He had been shown a film about Jesus in a private home and had been teaching villagers about the dangers of arsenic in water, mother-and-child health care and HIV/AIDS prevention.[14]

April 2010: Buddhist extremists took three Christian converts captive in the Chittagong Hills, forcing them to wear robes, shave their heads and honour the Buddha. Pastor Shushil Jibon Talukder, 55, Bimol Kanti Chakma, 50, and Laksmi Bilas Chakma, 40, all members of Maddha Lemuchari Baptist Church in Lemuchari village, in the mountainous Khagrachari district, south-east of Dhaka, were taken captive on 16th April. They were kept in a pagoda for 15 to 20 days as punishment for having left Buddhism.[15]

August-September 2010: The same Buddhist extremists responsible for April's attacks held a pastor and seven members of a Baptist church in the Chittagong Hills on the 23rd August. The Baptists were forced to wear Buddhist robes, shave their heads, bow down to a statue of the Buddha and help clean the temple. They were initially told they would be confined to the temple for a couple of weeks, but after four days they were released on the condition that they remained Buddhist.

October 2010: Christian convert Aynal Haque, 63, and his 22-year-old son Lal Miah were beaten by relatives and local Muslims on the 9th October when they refused to recant their faith. The family were living at Sadhu Hati Panta Para village in Jhenaidah district, about 155 miles (250 km) south-west of the capital. Villagers claimed he ate pork and trampled on the *Qur'an* to become Christian. He said: "I embraced Christianity by my own will and understanding, but I have due respect for other religions… Whatever rumours the villagers are spreading are false."[16]

December 2010: The United People's Democratic Front, a political party, ordered the leaders of churches including the Kalapani Bethlehem Church and the Chotopanchari Baptist Church not to hold Christmas celebrations. One pastor was ordered to revert to Buddhism.[17]

Belarus

Population	Religions	Christian Population
9.5 million	Christian 74% Non religious 25% Other 1%	7 million

Russian Orthodox faithful, Catholics, Lutherans, Jews and Muslims have continued to face problems in spite of a 2002 law recognising each religion as a "traditional faith". Foreign missionaries often confront administrative obstacles, especially concerning residence permits. The state often interferes in religious life: all faith activities and religious buildings require state approval and there is a ban on religious activity in most homes. [18]

Christian groups other than those mentioned above have experienced more problems. Their meetings have been raided, their property seized and they have been fined for 'unauthorised' religious activities. Dinas Linkus, Minsk's Deputy Chief of Frunze District Police, said: "We have Orthodox, Catholics and Muslims – these are the religions. All the others are sects."[19] 50 Protestant pastors – many of whom had been punished for religious activity – wrote to Belarus's President Alexander Lukashenko in August 2009 complaining about restrictions.[20] Prospects for improved treatment of Protestants and other Christians remained uncertain after Mr Lukashenko began a fourth term as president after much-disputed elections in December 2010 prompted clashes between security and opposition groups.

Property has remained a controversial issue. Although about 95 percent of historical Orthodox churches have been returned, Lutheran and Calvinist Christians have had little success. Permits to build new churches have been difficult to acquire. The state has revealed plans to transform a number of places of worship into hotels or museums, including the 17th century baroque Bernardine monastery in Minsk and the attached Church of St Joseph. However, following talks with President Lukashenko in April 2010, Archbishop Tadeusz Kondrusiewicz of Minsk-Mogilev, the head of the Catholic Church in Belarus, expressed the hope that problems with building new churches could be resolved.[21] In August 2010 the Church received permission to build several new shrines.[22] However, the state imposed tough quality control checks, causing building costs to rise dramatically. Observers said the president wanted the shrines to boost his prestige.

January 2009: The Catholic Church in Belarus appealed for the state to extend permits for four priests and three nuns working in the country. One of the priests, Fr Zbigniew Grygorcewicz, was told that he was being expelled for organising a Christian music festival.[23]

January 2009: The Higher Economic Court threw out Minsk's charismatic New Life Church's appeal against their building being seized by the state. The state argued that the building was a cowshed and hence was being illegally used for religious purposes. The church had unsuccessfully attempted to register a change of use.[24]

January 2009: Baptist leader Alexaander Yermalitsky was fined for hosting "a religious event at which the Bible was read" at his home.[25]

February 2009: Two Danish visitors were deported for expressing "ideas of a religious nature". The two were filmed actively participating in a service at Gomel's charismatic Living Faith Church.[26]

March 2009: A Belarusian Christian rehabilitation programme for alcoholics and drug addicts run by registered social organisation Cliff House was raided by police on two occasions, once when five participants were singing Christian songs.[27]

December 2009: Polish Catholic priests Fr Jan Bonkowski, who was parish priest of Mizhevitsi village for 20 years, and Fr Edward Smaga were told to stop all religious activity by the end of 2009.[28]

July 2010: Protestant pastor Viktor Novik was fined three times in one day for preaching outdoors in a village. Novik said he applied several times for permission, but this was disputed by local officials.[29]

July 2010: A Catholic festival was publicly celebrated on 1st-2nd July when Braslaw hosted festivities in honour of the Mother of God of Budslaw. Thousands participated with full approval of the authorities.[30]

December 2010: Bishop Alexander Kashkevich of Hrodna said that, despite an agreement having been prepared between President Lukashenko and the Vatican's secretary of state, Cardinal Tarcisio Bertone, the Catholic Church was still facing problems, especially obtaining visas for foreign priests.[31]

Bosnia–Herzegovina

Population	Religions	Christian Population
3.8 million	Muslim 55%	1.5 million
	Christian 41%	
	Other 4%	

Ethnic discrimination remains a serious problem, especially against non-Serbs in the country's predominantly Serb region, against non-Croats in western Herzegovina, and against non-Bosniaks in central Bosnia. In some regions, discrimination gives way to violence and other forms of abuse.

The line separating ethnic identity and religion is often blurred. Ethnic cleansing during the 1992-95 war caused vast numbers of people to be displaced and led to the population being segregated into separate areas. Although internal borders have since reopened, many – including a number of Catholics – have been reluctant to return to their former homes, which in numerous cases still lacked basic services including water and electricity.

Bosnia-Herzegovina is comprised of two essentially autonomous states: the Federation of Bosnia and Herzegovina and the Republic of Srpska. The majority of Serbian Orthodox live in the Republic of Srpska, and the majority of Muslims and Catholics reside in the Federation – with most Catholics living in Herzegovina and central Bosnia. Protestants and other minority religious groups tend to be concentrated in larger cities, such as Sarajevo, Banja Luka and Mostar.[32]

Leaders of religious minorities continue to complain about discrimination by local government officials. In particular Christians face difficulties using of their own properties for religious purposes. The Alliance of Protestant-Evangelical Churches in Bosnia and Herzegovina has experienced problems gaining registration. The Justice Ministry stated that this was because of the law's failure to recognise the term 'alliance'.

Church leaders and faithful have expressed concern about the radicalisation of Islam in the country. Reports suggest Bosnia-Herzegovina is a breeding ground for Islamist terrorists, alleging that more than 100,000 young Bosnian Muslims have been exposed to the extremist Wahabi vision of Islam through organisations such as Active Islamic Youth, Furqan, and the Muslim Youth Council. Reports suggest that in officially registered Muslim camps selected young men learn marksmanship and explosives training.[33]

Church leaders including Cardinal Vinko Puljic, Archbishop of Sarajevo, have complained of being given inadequate protection against harassment of Christians and vandalism of churches. Visiting Aid to the Church in Need's international headquarters in October 2010, Cardinal Puljic said his cathedral had recently come under attack from vandals and that such violence was commonplace. Some reports indicated that violence against Christians had declined but other sources showed that attacks on churches – both Orthodox and Catholic – remained a serious problem. In Sarajevo and elsewhere, the Catholic Church reported huge difficulties obtaining permission to build new churches despite increasing numbers of faithful.

January 2009: On the Orthodox Christmas Eve (6th January), unidentified arsonists burned the flag on the Orthodox cathedral in the Federation city of Tuzla. Police provided around-the-clock protection for the church.[34]

March 2009: St Luke's Catholic Church in the Municipality of Novi Grad, Sarajevo, suffered its 16th attack since 2005. During the week of the 23rd March the windows of the church were damaged three times. Police arrested a suspect, who admitted that he was responsible for two incidents, but did not file charges against him.[35]

August 2009: Two shots were fired at the Orthodox Church in the Reljevo suburb of Sarajevo. Police arrested an individual, who confessed to the crime and to being drunk at the time of the incident. The priest stated that this was the fifth attack on the church that year.[36]

September 2009: Catholics gathering for Mass at Londza cemetery near Donji Vakuf, in the Federation, were pelted with rocks by unidentified assailants. One woman suffered slight injuries. Police insisted the attackers were minors.[37]

October 2010: A former prisoner said organised Islamist groups inside Zenica prison were targeting Christian Croats and Serbs and claimed there was religious discrimination among prison authorities. He claimed many Muslim inmates receive better treatment: including Muamer Topalovic, a member of Bosnian organisation Active Islamic Youth. The former inmate said: "Topalovic, who murdered Croats at Christmas [2002] has the most superb treatment in the prison."[38]

Burma (Myanmar)

Population	Religions	Christian Pop.
50 million	Buddhist 80%	3 million
	Local religions 7%,	
	Christian 6%	
	Muslim 3.5% Other 3.5%	

When opposition leader Aung San Suu Kyi was released from house arrest in November 2010, it quickly became clear that Burma's military junta were in no mood to compromise and concede ground to pro-democracy campaigners. Their grip on power remained absolute despite widespread concern over the legitimacy of that month's general elections, which Suu Kyi's National League for Democracy party had boycotted. The vote – the first of its kind for 20 years – once again put the spotlight on Burma's poor human rights record. The ruling military junta passed a new constitution in 2008 which was quickly condemned by south-east Asia experts for its denial of human rights to particular ethnic groups. The criticisms of the 22-year-old regime focus on widespread abuse of civil liberties. Hopes of defeating oppression have been kept alive by Suu Kyi despite her lengthy detention by the authorities since the 1990 election which she won. Her outspoken defence of the Burmese people – as well as those of human rights organisations – have drawn the world's attention to the plight of people of all ethnicities and faiths, including Christians.

Both Catholic and Protestant communities are found in concentrated numbers among the ethnic Chin and Karen groups. They are labelled dissidents by the regime and hence suffer intimidation and outright persecution. Among the military operations carried out against ethnic minorities were the attacks of August 2009, an offensive which resulted in up to 40,000 people fleeing abroad. In addition mounting opposition to Christianity is visible in the forced closure of a large number of Protestant churches in 2010. The regime's determination to check the rise of Christianity attracted international attention in 2008 when it refused foreign aid following the devastating Cyclone Nargis. Fearful of international reaction to the severe poverty in Burma, the junta tried as much as possible to conceal the scale of the storm damage from the outside world. Some reports at the time suggested the government was suspicious that the emergency help was a front for covert Christian missionary work.

2009: A new law was adopted in effect banning independent 'house churches'. Many Christian groups were forced underground after the regime repeatedly blocked their applications for churches and chapels.

January 2009: Officials forced the closure of more than 100 churches in Rangoon and ordered owners of apartment buildings and conference facilities not to rent their properties to religious groups. According to Human Rights Watch, Burma's Chin people, who are reportedly up to 90 percent Christian, are the victims of serious and ongoing abuses. These include Christians being forced to provide funds for Buddhist pagodas. Sometimes they are forced to build the religious structures themselves. One Chin clergyman described how Burmese soldiers brought him to a pagoda and prodded him with their guns, commanding him to pray as a Buddhist.[39]

March 2010: On a fact-finding trip to the Thailand-Burma border in February 2010, Christian Solidarity Worldwide (CSW) discovered evidence of human rights abuse against the Karen people, a tribe with a high proportion of Christians. CSW documented firsthand testimonial evidence of widespread and systematic use of forced labour, torture and murder. CSW concluded that the violations amount to war crimes and crimes against humanity. The trip followed a CSW mission to Thailand in June 2009 where staff visited temporary camps for Karen refugees. Thai military attempted to deport the refugees forcibly back to Burma in areas infested with landmines and controlled by the Burma Army and its proxy militia. CSW witness statements showed people had been subjected to continuous harassment and pressure to return to Burma.[40]

October 2010: Christians from minority ethnic states described fears that after the November 2010 national elections, the military regime was set to 'cleanse' areas of Christianity. They reported that the Burmese Air Force had recently acquired military helicopters with a view to carrying out air strikes in high-density Christian areas in Kachin, in the far north, close to the Chinese border, and in Karen and Karenni states which are near the Thai border. The reports quoted a Burmese Air Force source who stated that the junta had designated many areas in the region as 'Black Zones', adding: "There are many unarmed Christian residents in these zones where Burmese military personnel attack and kill anyone in sight."[41]

China

Population	Religions	Christian Pop.
1.3 billion	Atheist 40% Chinese religions 35% Buddhist 12%, Christian 5%, Muslim 2%, Other 6%	65 million

China is a country of contradictions. With its economy growing rapidly, it is now one of the world's top exporters and attracts record amounts of foreign investment. While the global financial crisis of 2008-09 initially hit China hard, its economy was among the first to recover.[42] However, as the world's most populous nation has grown economically, embracing private enterprise, the regime continues to keep tight control over many aspects of society, strictly imposing one-party rule. This is one of the paradoxes of a country where members of the ruling Communist Party are strongly discouraged from participating in religious activities.

Some religious and spiritual groups are banned completely, including the Falun Gong. In some regions, including Tibet and the Xinjiang Uighur Autonomous Region, government repression of religious freedom was reported to have worsened, especially following unrest in March 2008 (Tibet) and July 2009 (Xinjiang).[43]

Despite the continuing tight controls concerning religious practice, reports suggest there is growing interest in religion, especially Christianity. According to statistics from China's State Administration for Religious Affairs in June 2010, there are now 16 million Protestants and more than 5.3 million Catholics worshipping in state-approved churches. However, unofficial estimates give much higher figures. The Pew Research Centre recently estimated that between 50 and 70 million Christians attend unregistered churches. The Holy Spirit Study Centre in Hong Kong gave a figure of 12 million Catholics but other sources suggest there could be many more.

Christianity's growth is set in the context of continuing difficulties overshadowing Church-state relations. The authorities still insist that Church communities be registered, a point of division, or at the very least tension, between Christian groups. Many state-recognised 'Official' Catholic communities are regulated by the Chinese Catholic Patriotic Association (CPA), an arm of government which seeks to control the

25

Church, most notably in the area of clergy appointments. In spite of their relationship with the state, the vast majority of 'Official' Church communities take loyalty to Rome just as seriously as their so-called 'Underground' Catholic co-religionists, who reject what they describe as unwarranted government interference. While only patriotic religious associations may register places of worship, the regime has not technically outlawed the 'Underground' Catholic Church and unregistered Protestant house churches. Rather, they are not permitted to hold public religious services.[44]

Restrictions on religious practice are enforced at a provincial level and are open to local interpretation, hence vastly different situations are experienced by 'Underground' and 'Official' Church communities across China's provinces. Unregistered Protestant communities continue to be raided and have their activities monitored or disrupted. While the vast majority are reported to be opposed to state registration, others have complained that when they tried to register, they were prevented from doing so by the Religious Affairs Office.

There were indications of improved relations between 'Underground' and 'Official' Catholics. In recent years many 'Official' Catholic bishops have discretely become reconciled with the Holy See. Benedict XVI's Letter to Chinese Catholics (27th May 2007) encouraged 'Official' and 'Underground' bishops to cooperate, and Cardinal Ivan Dias' letter of July 2010 was aimed at strengthening ties between the two groups.

Early on in the period under review, evidence suggested a softening of government attitudes towards the Church. For example in January 2009 the regime allowed a number of churches in Beijing to reopen – and indeed there were signs of improved relations with certain Churches not regulated by the state. However, in December 2010, the regime took bold steps to reassert its authority over the Catholic Church and supplant the role rightfully reserved for the Holy See. Reportedly using violence in some instances, state-registered bishops were forced to attend a meeting in Beijing to elect a new leadership of government-controlled Church organisations. The meeting resulted in the appointment of a bishop – not recognised by Rome – as president of the government-controlled College of Catholic Bishops of China. The Holy See responded by declaring that such developments were "unacceptable and hostile" to the Church. A Vatican communiqué declared that the methods used to convoke the assembly reflected "a repressive attitude with regard to the exercise of religious liberty, which it was hoped had been consigned to the past in present-day China".[45]

At the time of writing, several Catholic priests were still being held in prison or forced labour camps. In March 2009 Bishop Julius Jia Zhiguo of Zhending was arrested for the 13th time since 2004. He was released 15 months later.[46] Up to six bishops are under house-arrest. Of these, the whereabouts of two are still unknown after many years – 76-year-old Bishop James Su Zhimin of Baoding, who disappeared in 1996, and Bishop Cosmas Shi Enxiang, 87, of Yixian, who disappeared in 2001.

January 2009: The government announced plans to restore 12 places of worship in Beijing. The announcement was made by Beijing Religion Bureau official Yang Xiaodong. Wang Lei of the Beijing Catholic Association said: "The church in the heart of Changxindian township, home to about 200 Catholics, will make life easier for believers because they don't have to travel all the way to Xuanwumen Catholic Church to attend service."[47]

February 2009: Christian human rights activist and lawyer Gao Zhishen was seized by security agents. During his captivity, the China Aid Association released a letter written by him in 2007, chronicling a previous 50-day period of imprisonment. Gao described how officers urinated on him and repeatedly prodded his body, mouth and genitals with electric shock batons. Gao wrote that other methods used were too graphic and "horrible" to describe.[48]

February 2009: Chinese authorities continued to block Catholic websites, having targeted Catholic sites since the Vatican published the Compendium of Benedict XVI's May 2007 Letter to China on the Chinese section of its website.[49] In April 2009 the unregistered Shouwang Christian Church had its website forcibly shut down for being the "website of an illegal Christian organisation".

March 2009: Fr Francis Gao Jianli, 40, of the diocese of Fengxiang (Shaanxi), was beaten in connection with comments he made about a plot of land containing a former church that was seized by the authorities. The

27

mayor had invited Fr Gao to visit the town hall to discuss the land in Xiangong parish. After a heated debate, the mayor called in two men who beat up the priest so badly that he had to be taken to hospital. The land was seized during the Cultural Revolution (1966-76) to build a factory. The plant closed down some years ago and under Chinese law those who have rightful title to property can claim it back if it is not being used. There had been positive discussions between the Church and the district government's Property Management Office until the mayor decided to take the land to clear it to build a garden. Following a sit-in by parishioners on the site, the mayor then invited Fr Gao to discuss the matter.

March 2009: Restrictions were tightened on 'Underground' Catholic Churches in Hebei province (home to the highest concentration of Catholics in the country), as the Commission for the Catholic Church in China began its second meeting in the Vatican. In one incident, 55-year-old Fr Paul Ma was arrested for celebrating Mass with parishioners.[50]

March 2009: Rev "Bike" Zhang Mingxuan, leader of the Chinese House Church Alliance – which claims more than 250,000 members – was arrested by more than a dozen policemen at 6am. He was arrested in Yanjiao (Hebei), where he was staying overnight after conducting a baptism. Rev Zhnag claimed police threatened to kill him during his interrogation.

March 2009: 'Underground' Bishop Julius Jia Zhiguo of Zhengding, 74, was taken from his home by five police officers and placed in custody. He had previously been under 24-hour police surveillance to prevent him meeting with the CPA's Bishop Jang Taoran of Shijiazhuang (Hebei). Bishop Taoran is reconciled with the Holy See, and Bishop Jia Zhiguo was to become his auxiliary bishop, despite refusing to join the CPA himself. Bishop Jia has suffered health problems caused by previous incarcerations and old age. The Vatican's Commission on the Church in China issued a statement, expressing its "deepest regrets" over the arrest, highlighting the situation faced by other clerics "deprived of freedom".[51]

July 2009: 'Official' Catholic Bishop Joseph Li Shan of Beijing, whose appointment was approved by the Vatican, publicly defended the CPA's policy of Church self government, and upheld the separation of the Catholic Church in China from the Holy See. He denounced "divisions" between the 'Official' and 'Underground' Church caused by "anti-Chinese Western powers, which hurts evangelisation".[52]

July 2009: A Bible school in Suqian city, Jiangsu province, was raided. Pastor Shi Enhao and 11 students were taken to the Public Security Bureau office and questioned before being released later the same day. They were warned not to meet again.[53]

July 2009: Police arrested Fr Chen Hezhao, 40, an 'Underground' priest in Aoxin (Baoding). He had just come back from studying in France.

August 2009: A registered church in Rizhao City had the graduation ceremony of its church training school disrupted by officials from the City Bureau of Religious Affairs and Dongang police department. After seizing Bibles, computers, and other items, they revoked the church's registration.[54]

August 2009: Orthodox clergy consecrated the Church of St Innokenty of Irkutsk in the city of Labdarin, north China. It was the first time in 50 years that such a consecration had been held.[55]

September 2009: Up to 400 police officers and others descended on the Golden Lamp Church, built to hold nearly 50,000 worshippers, in the northern province of Shaanxi. They broke doors and windows, seized Bibles, removed computers, hospitalised dozens of worshippers who suffered serious injuries, and jailed the church's pastors. Officially the crackdown was the result of a land dispute, but the church was unregistered. Five church leaders were convicted of illegally occupying agricultural land and assembling a crowd to disrupt traffic. A lawyer for the defendants said the church had applied for building permits but received no reply.[56]

November 2009: Hundreds of Protestants met for Sunday worship in the snow in Haidian Park, Beijing after their landlord evicted them from their church, reportedly under pressure from the Beijing Bureau of Religious Affairs and Public Safety. The following Sunday the church's pastor, Jin Tianming, was detained by police for three hours.

December 2009: Bishop Leo Yao Liang, co-adjutor bishop of Xiwanzi (Hebei), died in hospital at the age of 86. Despite police being deployed to keep members of his 'Underground' diocese away from the funeral, and a

29

heavy snowfall, at least 5,000 people attended. Local authorities forced funeral organisers not to refer to his episcopal status and simply call him 'Pastor Yao'. However, during the burial, the faithful openly prayed for 'Bishop Yao' and some of the faithful placed his episcopal insignia in the coffin at the moment of burial. His death came a year after he was released from a three-year prison sentence.

December 2009-January 2010: In Xinjiang, a wave of persecution was carried out against Han and Uyghur Christians between Christmas and New Year. On Christmas Day, police burst into the home of 69-year-old He Cuiying, where several Christians were praying. Five elderly Christians were arrested and fined 5,000 yuan each before being released. Police also seized more than 30 Bibles.

January 2010: Xinjiang police detained 14 Christians in Aksu District. Nongwushi Police Chief Chen Xiaolong said: "They were questioned because they were meeting illegally. We advised them to go to a registered church instead." 11 of the group were held for more than 12 hours.

March 2010: Guangzhou police seized Liangren Church's Head Pastor Wang Dao while he was eating in a restaurant with 12 members of his congregation. After throwing him to the floor, police took Pastor Wang outside to a waiting vehicle. Six months earlier, Pastor Wang had been questioned by police for more than three hours.[57]

April 2010: Bishop Matthias Du Jiang, 47, of Bameng in Inner Mongolia, was placed under police observation after refusing to concelebrate Mass with Bishop Ma Yinglin, CPA vice-chairman. 'Underground' Bishop Du was to be 'officially' installed and have his clandestine consecration recognised by the government, but initially refused to concelebrate with Bishop Ma, who was ordained without Vatican approval. However under pressure from the CPA, Bishop Du went ahead with the official installation ceremony at Sanshenggong Cathedral with Bishop Ma in attendance but not presiding. Bishop Ma Yinglin sat with the priests. In his homily, Bishop Du openly thanked the Pope for appointing him to the Diocese of Bameng.[58]

May 2010: Up to eight plain-clothes police officers raided the Sunday service at Chimei Town House Church in Neixiang county, Nanyang, Henan province, photographing, fingerprinting, and registering the 20-

strong congregation before taking nine people into custody, including a four-year-old boy. The boy and his mother were released, but the others were given sentences ranging from five to 15 days.[59]

June 2010: A Beijing court found Christian bookshop owner Shi Weihan guilty of an "illegal business operation", sentencing him to three years in prison and a 150,000 yuan (US$21,975) fine. Shi had been printing Bibles and Christian literature for free distribution to local house churches. After a previous arrest, 38-year-old Shi had been released on 4th January 2008 because of insufficient evidence against him. However he was arrested again two months later. The publication of Bibles comes under the jurisdiction of the State Administration for Religious Affairs. Selling Bibles is only permitted by government-authorised Churches. Many Christian communities have printed and imported millions of copies of Bibles into China.[60]

July 2010: 75-year-old Bishop Julius Jia Zhiguo of Zhengding, who was arrested in March 2009, was released from prison. Soon after his release, Bishop Jia celebrated Mass and made it clear that he had not joined the CPA during his imprisonment.[61]

July 2010: Newly appointed Bishop Antonio Xu Jiwei, 75, who was consecrated bishop of Taizhou, in Zhejiang province, said he was "optimistic about a revival of evangelisation and a growth of the Catholic community". The see of Taizhou had been vacant since 1962. The new bishop was approved by both the Holy See and government authorities.[62]

November 2010: The Holy Father expressed his regret over the illicit episcopal ordination of Joseph Guo Jincai. He said the ordination in Chengde, Hebei province, was "a painful wound upon ecclesial communion and a grave violation of Catholic discipline".[63]

December 2010: Catholic Church sources said that 'Official' bishops and priests were deported to the capital to take part in meetings to appoint leaders of government-controlled Church assemblies. *AsiaNews* reported that many bishops were desperate to avoid attending the meetings and went into hiding or declared themselves too ill to attend. In Henshui diocese, Hebei, Bishop Feng Xinmao was seized by about 100 police officers and government representatives who fought for hours against the faithful and priests who were shielding their bishop.[64]

Cuba

Population	Religions	Christian Population
11.3 million	Christian 70% Atheist 15% Local religions 15%	7 million

The decision by Cuba's communist regime in late 2009 to lift the ban on church services in the country's prisons was seen by many human rights observers as symptomatic of improved Church-state relations. Much has changed in Cuba since the early 1960s, when the new President Fidel Castro declared his communist regime to be atheist and ordered a crackdown on the Church. Religious buildings were seized, Catholic schools were closed and priests were expelled. Signs of change came in 1997 when, in the run-up to Pope John Paul II's state visit to Cuba, the regime lifted the ban on Christmas celebrations and travel restrictions were eased for clergy.

Since Raul Castro took over as President from his brother in February 2008, it would appear that improvements – at least for the Catholic Church – have gathered apace. In an unprecedented development, a nationwide appeal got underway in 2009 to raise funds for Cuba's national shrine of Our Lady of Charity of Cobre, in preparation for a national pilgrimage in 2010 and 400th anniversary celebrations of the image in 2012. The growing activities surrounding Our Lady of Cobre are seen by Cuba observers as significant for two main reasons. First, celebrations associated with Cuba's patron were banned until as late as 1997. Secondly, it has historically been very difficult to obtain official permission to hold processions and activities outside religious buildings.

Also, during successive years, Cardinal Jaime Ortega, Archbishop of Havana, has been able to broadcast his Christmas message on state television, another indication of improving relations with the government.

In a sign that the Church is at last emerging from the shadows, Cardinal Ortega gave probably his most forthright criticism of the regime. In an April 2010 interview he said the government faced open criticism in the streets and that the country was facing its worst economic and social crisis. By then it was being reported that the government was encouraging Cardinal Ortega to lobby the US to end its trade embargo of Cuba. The

Church was seen to be playing a potentially important role in the government's struggle against deepening poverty. At about this time, Cardinal Ortega intervened after police broke up demonstrations by the 'Ladies in White' – wives and mothers of political demonstrators. The government duly allowed the marches to go ahead.

In July 2010 the regime agreed to free 52 political detainees in the largest prisoner release by the communist authorities for decades. The agreement to release the prisoners came after talks between President Raul Castro and Cardinal Ortega. The communist government openly recognised the local Cuban Church as an intermediary and mediator in social and political issues.

Nevertheless there are still many areas – such as education, health and social services – in which the Catholic Church and other Christian groups are not allowed to work or be involved. Indeed not everything is pointing to change for the better. Religious rights organisations report that Cuba continues to harass Christian groups not recognised by the state and media access is often limited. Lay faithful continue to face discrimination in the workplace, apparently for religious reasons. There is still no major break-through in the return of Church buildings confiscated by the regime 40 years ago.

While it is beyond doubt that the Catholic Church's position has improved, Cuba observers have raised questions about the extent of change in government thinking, suggesting that the progress could be short term and easily put into reverse. Other Christian denominations have not benefited as much from the thaw in official attitudes to religious practice. Unregistered Christian communities have reported that the government continues to destroy 'house churches', sometimes arresting their members and imposing heavy fines. Meanwhile all Christian communities have voiced concerns of an upsurge in monitoring by Cuba's surveillance services.

December 2009: Pope Benedict XVI expressed his hope that "concrete signs of openness to the exercise of religious freedom [in Cuba] will continue to multiply as they have in recent years".

April 2010: Cardinal Ortega called for the release of all political prisoners, including large numbers of Christians jailed for religious activities. Calling

33

for the government to make the changes "quickly", Cardinal Ortega said the people were openly discussing the deficiencies of Cuba's socialist system, which he described as being a Stalinist-style bureaucracy. He referred to the recent death of a dissident hunger-striker in jail and the harassment of the 'Ladies in White' as "distressing".[65]

April 2010: Up to 3,000 Christians took to the streets of the city of Santa Clara on Easter Sunday morning in a spontaneous celebration. It began when a clergyman leading a service in his church suddenly suggested that the people join him in a procession outside the church. Almost 10 churches took part. They walked for over a mile (2 km) through the city and observers said the police made no attempt to break up the procession.[66]

August 2010: While acknowledging signs of improvements for many Christian communities in Cuba, Christian Solidarity Worldwide (CSW) reported that the communist regime remains inflexible in key areas of religious freedom. CSW's August 2010 report *Religious freedom in Cuba* cites evidence showing "frequent" visits to churches by security staff and government officials, who reportedly appeared intent on "intimidating Church leaders". The government's so-called Office of Religious Affairs has reportedly blocked many religious activities and has denied exit visas for clergy wanting to travel abroad. The report concluded: "Rather than moving towards a more open society, the government of Raul Castro still views religious organisations, and in particular their leaders, as potentially dangerous, and as a result continues to exert as much control as possible over their activities."[67]

October 2010: Evangelical Christians in Cuba grew in number from 70,000 to 800,000 within 20 years, according to Cuba's Council of Churches. The Catholic Church and Afro-Cuban religious traditions also attracted large numbers of new faithful. Evangelical Christianity is now thought to be the fastest-growing religious group. Reports strongly indicate that at a time of increasing economic hardship, people are turning to faith in search of hope and help.[68]

November 2010: Cuban President Raul Castro attended the inauguration of a new national Catholic seminary on the outskirts of Havana, the first new Catholic building on the communist island in more than 50 years. Present at the ceremony was a US archbishop, Vatican officials, as well as Cuban clergy.[69]

Democratic Republic of the Congo

Population	Religions	Christian Population
1.9 million	Christian 95.5% Local religions 2.5% Other 2%	1.8 million

Although religion has played little part in the continuing violence taking place in DR Congo, priests, religious Sisters and children in Christian schools have been the innocent victims of some of Africa's most savage crimes. As the country marked the 50th anniversary of independence in summer 2010, peace seemed as elusive as ever, especially in some regions. Armed groups, led by some of the continent's most deadly subterranean militia, have wreaked havoc and devastation. The US State Department's Human Rights report stated that the government increasingly had "weak control over many areas", that armed forces were "acting with impunity" and were responsible for unlawful killings, disappearances, arrests, and recruitment of child soldiers.[70]

The country's two million displaced people – nearly 75 percent of them in the Kivu region – were easy prey. Of this large number, 120,000 homeless people were supported by the Church and hence clergy have been inevitable targets. The brutal killing of a priest and a religious Sister in a Trappist monastery near Bukavu in late 2009 seemed to be a deliberate attack on the Church itself. Violence of a uniquely savage kind was the distinctive hallmark of so many groups terrorising the region. This was one of a number of reasons why the DR Congo government struggled to overpower the Democratic Forces for the Liberation of Rwanda – a Rwandan rebel group in the east of the country. By contrast, the regime has enjoyed more success against the Ugandan based Lords Resistance Army (LRA). But even with the LRA, the government suffered serious setbacks. When 300 civilians were killed in December 2009 in Makombo, north-east Congo, the rebels proved they still had the capacity to carry out violence on a massive scale. Recent statements from Church leaders show they were expecting no imminent breakthrough in the struggle against child abductions, pillaging and rape. Uncertainty and fear continued to beset the lives of many people – Christian and non-Christian alike.

January 2009: The Lords Resistance Army torched a church crowded with worshippers during a prayer vigil. The attack, on 17th January, took place close to the Sudanese border, not far from the military base of the multi-national offensive against the rebels. A local government official said: "The LRA entered the Church around midnight. They surprised the faithful who were in a prayer vigil. They burned them in the church." Details concerning the number of dead and injured were not confirmed.[71]

May 2009: Nearly 100 people died, including 25 children, in attacks in Busurungi, North Kivu, targeting several churches and schools as well as 700 homes and three health centres. The violence was carried out by about 7,000 fighters but the faction to which they belonged remained unclear.[72]

December 2009: Fr Daniel Cizimya Nakamaga, 51, was shot in the head when gunmen broke into his presbytery during the night in Kabare, outside Bukavu, a city in the east of the country. Less than 48 hours later attackers struck at a Trappist monastery, not far away from the previous attack, killing Sister Denise Kahambu. Sr Denise, who was the monastery's guest mistress, opened the door to strangers. An armed man chased her and she shouted for help. She was discovered "lying in a pool of blood". The rest of the nuns took shelter in the monastery dormitory, sitting on the floor in case shots were fired through the windows. Fr Crispin, rector of a nearby seminary, said later: "The whole time, the Sisters prayed the rosary and sang Psalm 129, the De Profundis, for Sr Denise and the whole community. The vicar general of the diocese of Bukavu, Mgr Pierre Bulambo, reported that police were continuing their investigations but hinted at possible collusion between security staff officials and the attackers.[73]

November 2010: A man in military uniform in an eastern province of DR Congo killed Fr Christian Mbusa Bakulene, parish priest of St John the Baptist's Church, Kanyabayonga, in the province of North Kivu. The incident on 8th November took place as the priest and a parish worker were on a motorbike returning to the parish. Two men in military uniform stopped the pair near the base of the Congolese Armed Forces. One of the 'soldiers' asked them: "Which of you is the priest?" Fr Bakulene replied: "I am." The gunman then took money from the companion before firing several shots, killing the priest. His companion was unharmed. According to *Fides* news agency, the attack was a "targeted killing [aimed at] frightening priests working in the area".[74]

Egypt

Population	Religions	Christian Population
84.5 million	Muslim 87.5% Christian 12% Other 0.5%	10 million

The Egyptian government's growing crackdown on the banned extremist political movement, the Muslim Brotherhood, is seen by many critics as indicative of the country's increasingly fraught struggle with militant Islam. Intense speculation over whether long-serving President Hosni Mubarak would stand again in the 2011 elections – amid reports of ill-health – only exacerbated tensions over the role of Islam in law and government. Egypt commentators raised concerns that to appease an increasingly active radical movement, the regime would have no option but to embrace a more hard-line Islamic model of governance, complete with greater reliance on *Shari'a*.

For the time being, however, the authorities have taken strong steps to check the rise of Islamism. As well as arresting dozens of Muslim Brotherhood members, the government took the controversial step of suspending 12 television stations for promoting religious hatred and violence. It coincided with a surge in reports of violence and other acts of intolerance against Christians. At about 10 million strong, there are far more Christians in Egypt than in any other country in the Middle East, a fact which explains the hostility they encounter in a country proud of its strong Islamic heritage.

Concern about the growth of extremism in Egypt became a matter of international public debate in January 2010, when extremists disrupted an Orthodox Coptic Christmas Midnight Mass in a shooting spree in which nine people died. The attack took place outside Mar Girgis (Saint George) Church in Nag-Hammadi (Upper Egypt), 30 miles (48 km) from Luxor. In another sign of worsening attitudes towards Christians, there has been a surge in abductions of young Coptic women and girls in order to force them to marry Muslim men. Conversion to Christianity remains unlawful, even though Article 46 of the Constitution says that the state guarantees freedom of belief and religion. In fact, the courts tend to enforce *Shari'a*. Therefore, according to the Vital Statistics Office, a Muslim who is baptised a Christian is still a Muslim. This means that a former Muslim cannot change his or her identity papers to show a new religion or name. In fact, the lack of a law on conversion from Islam to another religion leaves the matter in the hands of judges, who must choose between *Shari'a* and the principle of equality of all citizens before the law.

Interest in, and conversions to, Christianity continue to grow in spite of obvious risks to the safety of individuals, their families and property. This factor, alongside the popular linking of Christianity to the West, frequently demonised in popular culture, goes some way to explain the growing climate of opposition to the faithful of all Christian traditions – Orthodox, Catholic and Protestant alike. Apparently drawing on growing popular support, extremists are responding to reports of conversions to Christianity by stoking fears about Christians carrying out clandestine evangelisation work. Similarly, spurred on by militant imams, extremists have shown increased determination to crack down on the illegal construction of churches. Official permission for new churches can take up to 30 years and needs the personal approval of the President himself.

April-May 2009: At the height of the Swine Flu Pandemic, the Egyptian government ordered the slaughter of the country's 300,000 pigs. The decision immediately drew criticism from the World Health Organisation, which said that the virus was spread through humans. Other commentators also said that in any event no case of the virus had yet been reported in Egypt. Human rights and religious freedom organisations, noting the Muslim objection to pigs for religious reasons, pointed out that most pig farmers in the country were Christian. Egyptian animal-rights activist Amina Abaza deplored the slaughter of pigs and said "the decision to cull them was probably taken only because they belong to the Christians".

June 2009: In Qalubiya Province north of Cairo, a 60-year-old Christian man was beaten to death by a young Muslim man, aged 24. The victim's son was suspected of having had a relationship with the murderer's sister.

June 2009: Muslims attacked Coptic residents in the village of Ezbet Bouchra-East, destroying their homes and harvests. Their violence was prompted by the arrival of 25 Christians from Cairo to visit a local priest, Fr Isaac Castor, who lived in a building owned by the Coptic Church. From this, the Muslims had inferred that the Christian visitors had come to take part in a religious celebration. 19 Christians were later arrested but they were released the next day.

September 2009: In the regions of Assuan, Daqahlîya, Red Sea and Port Said, 150 Christians were arrested for "publicly breaking the Ramadan fast", i.e. eating or smoking in the street before sundown. Most were released from prison after paying a fine of 500 Egyptian pounds (US$100). For Samuel Alashay, director of a liberal Christian movement, this arrest, a first in Egypt, could be a response to a strike held on 11 September by a significant number of Copts demanding a law that would make it easier to build churches. The strike action came about following a fatwa (religious edict) issued by the Islamic Council of Egypt stating, "It is a sin against God for a Muslim to donate money for the construction of a church."

January 2010: At the end of Midnight Mass on 7th January 2010 (Christmas according to the Orthodox calendar), a number of Copts were gunned down as they left Mar Girgis (Saint George) Church in Nag-Hammadi (Upper Egypt), 25 miles (40 km) from Luxor. A car pulled up in front of the church, three men got out and began spraying the worshippers with bullets as they came out of the church. At least seven people were killed, including a police officer. A dozen were wounded, including two Muslims. The massacre was said to be an act of vengeance for the rape of a 12-year-old Muslim girl allegedly committed by a Copt in Farshout, near Nag-Hammadi, in November 2009. A 21-year-old Coptic man was arrested in connection with that case but his guilt remained in doubt. As reprisals, Muslims looted and set fire to shops and houses owned by Christians. About 80 percent of the shops attacked were destroyed. Some Christians were wounded and seven Christian women were abducted. Police only moved in after the attack. Local authorities called on Christian victims not to file a complaint and instead seek some form of compromise with the Muslim attackers. None of the Christians has received any compensation.

January 2010: Egyptian Coptic Orthodox leader Pope Shenouda III called on Egyptian courts to step up efforts to bring the murderers of Christians to justice. It is alleged that over the past 30 years, some 1,800 Christians have been murdered and 200 acts of vandalism have been perpetrated against Christian property, with few if any court convictions.

March 2010: A court in Assiut acquitted four Muslims accused of killing a Christian in October 2009. The court's decision caused shock as there were reportedly a number of witnesses to the murder and the attack was particularly brutal. The victim, Atallah Farouk, was shot in the head several times, before being beheaded. His body was dragged through the streets and his alleged killers shouted "Victory". In its ruling, the court refused to take into account the testimony of the victim's daughter and that of a man wounded by gunshots during the attack. Local media reported that most other witnesses refused to testify for fear of reprisal. Lawyer Peter Sarwar, acting on behalf of the victim's family, said: "This verdict sends out a message that a Copt's blood is extremely cheap." Afterwards, he immediately launched an appeal.

March 2010: 25 people, including women and children, were wounded when a 3,000 strong crowd disrupted a Coptic Christian service in Mersa Matrouh, a coastal town west of Alexandria. More than 400 parishioners, including four priests, had gathered at the site of a proposed nursing home for a prayer service, when the group of Muslim fanatics – Bedouins and Salafis – started throwing stones at the walls of the unfinished building. One Christian, a teacher called Mounir Naguib, said he was stopped by the mob when he was on his way to the service and pressured to convert to Islam. He was stabbed in the leg when he refused. The extremists believed the new structure was going to be a church, but the Church authorities stated it was to be a nursing home. Local witnesses reported that the security forces present were not strong enough to stop the violence and a number of worshippers were trapped inside the building. They only escaped when security reinforcements arrived the next day from Alexandria. It is claimed that the attack followed a statement by the local imam, Shaikh Khamees, who at Friday Prayers called on Muslims to fight against the "enemies" of Islam, stressing "we do not tolerate the Christian presence in our area".[75]

September 2010: Coptic Catholic Bishop Joannes Zakaria appealed for prayers following a succession of suspicious fires in church buildings. In the latest incident, the Coptic Catholic church in Hagazah village was completely destroyed by a blaze. The bishop explained that he had been told by government and police authorities that the likely cause of the fire was a short circuit. He added: "During the meeting, I asked permission to prepare a building to celebrate the holy Mass next Sunday for about 600 Coptic Catholics who live in the village but they refused."[76]

November 2010: Work was nearing completion on a new church, near the Pyramids, when the government intervened to stop the work. Police surrounded SS Michael and Mary's Church, in Talbiya, Giza, during the night. Inside the church compound were thousands of Coptic Christians who had anticipated the security forces' arrival and who were taking part in a prayer vigil. They were outraged by the government decision, arguing that the church construction plan had received state approval. The church was close to completion with only the domes still unfinished. They also said the million-strong Copts had no other church in the Talbiya area. Samira Ibrahim Shehata, a volunteer worker at the church, said: "I want to know why a hundred mosques can be built and not one church." Responding to the police intervention, thousands of Copts surrounded the governorate of Giza and in the clashes two young Copts were killed and about 50 were injured. The local authorities were accused of creating excuses to stop the building work. It was alleged they had given in to demands from Muslim fundamentalists. Naguib Ghobrial, president of the Egyptian Union of Human Rights, called for the dismissal of the local government in Omraniya. Mr Ghobrial said: "The Church has all the permits [needed for the new church]. By this behaviour, the chief of the local authority is encouraging Islamists to fight with Christians."[77]

January 2011: More than 20 Massgoers died and at least 70 others were wounded when a car bomb exploded outside the Church of Saints, a Coptic Orthodox church, in Alexandria's Sidi Bechr district. The explosion took place while 1,000 people were attending Mass to celebrate the New Year. The incident sparked clashes between Muslims and Christians. Muslims accused the Egyptian Copitc Church and Patriarch Shenouda III of holding two women who converted to Islam captive against their will. This accusation, which was widely condemned as false, was repeated on the night of the attack in a mosque 200 meters from the Church of Saints. The terrorists who claimed responsibility for the October 2010 Baghdad massacre at the Syrian Catholic Cathedral, cited the same case of the two women to justify attacks on Christians in Egypt.[78]

January 2011: An off-duty policeman shot dead Fathi Saeed Ebaid, 71, and wounded his wife and four other Christians, on the train to Cairo. It is not known why Amer Ashour Abdel Zaher, opened fire. He was arrested following the incident.[79]

41

Profile: Bishop Kyrillos William of Assiut, Egypt

"In my diocese, I have a request for a church to be built that dates back 22 years. We are still waiting."

Describing the situation for Christians across Egypt, Bishop Kyrillos William said the reason for such a delay is simple: each request for the construction of a new church has to be approved personally by the President of Egypt.

Bishop Kyrillos goes on to give a list of similar problems that beg the question: how can the Church survive in such circumstances?

After 20 years based in the city of Assiut on the River Nile, about 232 miles (375 km) south of Cairo, it seems that Bishop Kyrillos has mastered the art of survival. Such are the essential life skills for Christians not just in Assiut diocese but all over Egypt.

While some church projects get no further than the drawing board, others are brought to completion through a careful balancing act involving diplomacy and improvisation. Bishop Kyrillos said that sometimes it was possible to obtain authorisation after a church is built. But more often than not, such a strategy can easily backfire. In Egypt there are many churches that have the appearance of a domestic home. To a casual observer, their true identity is completely unknown.

The gap between the letter of the law and day-to-day reality differs hugely from place to place. But what changes the situation more than anything else is the sheer number of Christians – perhaps 10 million in a population totalling more than 84 million. Whatever the precise number, it is undisputed that numerically this is by far the largest Church in the whole of the Middle East. That presence is strengthened by the deep historical roots of the Catholic and Orthodox Coptic Churches which date back before the coming of Islam in the 7th century when Egypt was a powerhouse of Christianity.

But all that is in the past. According to Bishop Kyrillos, the sheer size of the Christian presence in Egypt is deeply abhorrent to many sections of Egyptian society.

He goes on: "The media is full of attacks on Christians. They say they have to combat us, that we're not reliable, that we're not loyal to the country."

The bishop, who went to Rome for further studies in theology and philosophy, goes on to make clear that a culture of discrimination runs through the schools system. "In schools there are programmes intended to attack Christians. Teachers will say to Christian students that when they grow up they will be attacked."

He described instances where young Christian girls begin a relationship with a Muslim only to be abducted by the young man's family. They force her to convert and then proceed with the wedding plans regardless of her views or that of the family. Such incidents can cause serious tension in villages and towns, sometimes sparking violence.

A climate of intimidation and oppression towards Christians has grown dramatically, according to Bishop Kyrillos. He said: "The last 30-40 years has seen a spirit of fundamentalism become increasingly strong. There are people who simply cannot accept that there are Christians in Egypt. The fundamentalists are growing in number and are more organised. They do not allow people to take a different approach to them and they are very active."

The bishop also said that in mosques there is frequent criticism of Christianity. "On Fridays, imams always speak against the other religions. It is very painful. They look at Christian teachings and say what we believe is not true. They criticise the moral life of Christians."

The bishop himself knows what the pressure can be like. He recalled his young days doing compulsory military service under the post-war Egyptian president, Gamal Abdel Nasser. "I hadn't any problems standing up for my beliefs because my faith was strong," he said.

But for many, especially today, the pressure can prove too much. Bishop Kyrillos explained how the process of Islamisation was encouraging many Christians to emigrate. "Many Christians want to leave for the West – Australia and the USA. They want to find security. Emigration is a big, big problem for us – a problem for the Church across the Middle East."

He referred to the shock that echoed across Egypt and beyond in January 2010 when at least seven Christians were killed in the town of Nag

Hammadi, in the south of the country. The extremists opened fire on a group of worshippers leaving a Coptic Orthodox church after Christmas celebrations.

But in spite of the growing problems and the increasing tensions on both sides, the bishop was able to report that the climate of intolerance had in fact strengthened the people's faith. He said: "Christians are growing in faith and becoming closer to the Church. More people are coming to Church – we see this more and more."

He reported a massive increase in the number of pilgrims to Deir Dronka, the diocesan shrine, 7 km south of Assiut city. "Now we get two million coming to the shrine. The whole village is Christian so people like to come because it's somewhere where they can feel free – make processions, sing hymns."

He said that in these times of suffering, the faith of the people was an "impressive witness" to Christ.

Eritrea

Population	Religions	Christian Pop.
5 million	Muslim 50% Orthodox 40% Catholic 5% Protestant 2%, Other 3%	2.5 million

Noting "particularly severe violations of religious freedom", in early 2009, the US Secretary of State designated Eritrea as a 'Country of Particular Concern'.[80] Nearly two years later, the US State Department's official report on religious freedom showed that severe abuses against religious groups were unrelenting. Reports gave evidence of harassment, indefinite detention without charge, arrests during religious services as well as "forced recantations of faith and torture of religious prisoners".[81]

A 1995 government decree on authorised religions only recognises the Eritrean Coptic Orthodox Church, the Evangelical Lutheran Church, the Catholic Church and Islam.[82] Authorised denominations still need permission from the Office of Religious Affairs to publish documents and hold services or other activities. Church leaders and media are not allowed to comment on political issues. The construction of churches requires government approval.

State interference in the internal affairs of the Orthodox, Lutheran and Muslim communities is routine and the government has placed men loyal to the regime at the top of their hierarchies. Many Eritrean clergy and faithful do not recognise the new Patriarch Dioskoros, following reports of government interference in his appointment. The Catholic Church remains autonomous, but faces restrictions. Between 2007 and 2008, 18 Catholic missionaries did not have residency visas renewed, and since 2006, Eritrean priests have not been allowed to study in Rome or do missionary work abroad. The Catholic hierarchy has successfully resisted attempts to seize schools and other welfare projects – a 1995 decree reserved all social activities to the state – the most recent attempt being in 2007.

Since 2002, all unauthorised religious communities have been required to file registration requests giving details of their history in Eritrea, their leaders' names, property and other assets, as well as funds received from abroad. Several religious groups have applied but none has yet obtained government approval, despite reports showing they met the criteria.[83] Non-

45

recognised religious groups have been subject to continuing government arrests and detention without formal charge or trial.[84] Police have been repeatedly setting conditions for their release such as forcing members of these groups to sign declarations renouncing their faith and stating their intention to join the Eritrean Orthodox Church.

The most recent reports showed that there were probably more than 3,000 Christians imprisoned for their faith. Many were being held in underground cells or transport containers. The government opened a camp for religious prisoners in the desert near Mitire (Meiter) in north-eastern Eritrea. Reports showed that often prisoners were denied access to their family. Although many were accused of evading conscription, many were being held solely for their religious beliefs. Evidence points strongly to prisoners dying from torture and lack of medical attention.

One reason given for the arrests is a failure to do military service, which is compulsory for young people across the country. The government has a zero-tolerance policy towards conscientious objectors. That said, in 2008 Catholic seminarians were given an exemption from the service but it was due to expire by 2011. There had been reports that seminarians forced into doing a year's military service in 2008 were still at the training camps more than two years later. Eritrea observers suggest the government's insistence on military service is linked to its efforts to tackle emigration, especially among the young. With the country's deepening economic crisis making living conditions steadily worse, reports from Eritrea suggest people have been fleeing the country in unprecedented numbers. It is thought that there are 40,000 Eritreans in refugee camps in Ethiopia and up to 400,000 in Sudan.

January 2009: Three Christians incarcerated in military prisons for their faith died between October 2008 and January 2009. Mehari Gebreneguse Asgedom, 42, died at the Mitire Military Confinement centre from torture and complications from diabetes. Mogos Hagos Kiflom, 37, was said to have died as a result of torture he endured for refusing to recant his faith. Teklesenbet Gebreab Kiflom, 36, died while imprisoned for his faith at the Wi'a Military Confinement centre. He was reported to have died after prison commanders refused to give him medical attention for malaria.[85]

January 2009: Security forces arrested 27 Christians from the Rhema Church during a Sunday service on 25th January in Assab. They were beaten during their first days of detention. Their arrests brought to around 300 the number of members of the non-authorised groups arrested from the beginning of October 2008 to the end of January 2009.

April 2009: Christian charity Open Doors expressed concern over the EU's €122 million aid allocation to Eritrea in the face of the ongoing detainment of Christians in military prisons, labour camps, and metal shipping containers.[86]

June 2009: Security forces arrested 15 Orthodox monks in the chapel of Saint Mary in Asmara. A public meeting, led by Fr Gebretensai Hadegu, was being held there, denouncing government interference in the internal affairs of the Coptic Orthodox Church. Those arrested were taken to the Mitire Military Confinement centre.

June 2009: Four young Christians died after being kept in an underground cell at Assab, on the west coast of the Red Sea, for nearly six years. Temperatures in Assab reach 49°C (120°F) during the dry season. Reportedly there are several holes in the desert where Christians are kept, who only receive three pieces of bread, a cup of tea in the morning and three cups of water a day.[87]

September 2009: The Eritrean government called on citizens to inform the police of any illegal gatherings of Christians. Authorities said meetings by unregistered groups in private homes were criminal acts.[88]

September 2009: At least seven prisoners held at Wi'a Military camp died following an outbreak of meningitis, including Evangelical Christian Mesfin Gebrekristos who was arrested in 2007 for being a member of an unregistered Church.[89]

October 2009: Eritrean security forces raided the home of Tewelde Hailom, founder and Pastor of the Full Gospel Church in Asmara. Three people were arrested during the raid on 14th October. Pastor Hailom was placed under house arrest with guards positioned outside his home. Seven more people from his congregation were arrested on 16th October. Six days later a further three people linked to these arrests were detained.[90]

December 2009: 30 elderly Christian women were arrested on 5th

47

December for praying together at a private house in Asmara. Most of those detained were members of Faith Mission Church, an Evangelical Church with Methodist roots. 10 days later they were released.[91]

December 2009/January 2010: Fr Berhane Haileab of the Eritrean Orthodox Church in Nairobi, Kenya, was removed from his post. In December 2009 he received a demand to step down from state-appointed Church administrator Yoftahe Dimetros but he refused to return to Eritrea after questioning Yoftahe's authority. On January 3rd 2010 Fr Berhane's residence was broken into and his belongings removed. He was barred from entering the church and, after receiving death threats, went into hiding.[92]

January 2010: On the 24th, Hana Hagos Asgedom, 41, died of a heart attack while in an isolation cell in Alla military camp. She was a member of the Asabe Rhema Church. Arrested three years earlier and interned in the military prison of Wi'a, Hana had recently been transferred to Alla after refusing to abandon her religious beliefs. She was allegedly beaten with an iron bar shortly before her death for having refused sexual advances from the camp commander. On the 16th another religious prisoner, Mehari Gebreneguse Asgedom, 42, died at the Mitire camp.

February 2010: Eritrean authorities released 14 Christians who had spent the last two years in military camps. Twelve young Christians were released from Adi-Nefase camp, in the southern port city of Assab. All 12 were members of the Kale-Hiwot Church and were high school students at the time of their arrest. Two other Eritrean Christians, members of the Rhema Church in Adi-Kuala imprisoned for evangelising fellow soldiers, were released on bail from Mitire camp.[93]

March 2010: In the years since the Eritrean Government revoked the exemption of Orthodox clergy from military service in July 2005, over 1,400 have been conscripted. Many churches in rural Eritrea reported a severe shortage of clergy.[94]

March 2010: Military officials arrested 17 men at a prayer meeting in Segenaite, southern Eritrea. Reports suggested the men were soldiers doing national service, who belonged to several different Evangelical groups.[95]

March 2010: Efrem Habtemichel Hagos, 37, who belonged to a non-recognised Church, died in isolation in the military camp at Adi-Nefase near Assab, after suffering from malaria and pneumonia for three months.

He had previously been denied medical care for refusing to renounce his faith.

April 2010: 28-year-old female university student Senait Oqbazgi Habta died of malaria and anaemia at the health facility of the prison at the military training centre in Sawa. Habta was arrested in 2008 together with 15 other students from the Mai-Nehfi University for belonging to a Bible study group. Students were imprisoned in containers exposed to the hot sun during the day and the cold at night, without toilet facilities or medical care. Previously she had refused to sign a document renouncing her faith.

May 2010: 11 Christians belonging to the Faith Church of Christ were arrested, including women and children. They were attending a prayer meeting in a private house in Asmara when they were seized.[96]

July 2010: Yemane Kahasay Andom, 43, died at Mitire Military Confinement centre. Reports suggest he was secretly buried in the camp. Weakened by physical torture and solitary confinement in an underground cell for two weeks, Andom, a member of the Kale-Hiwot church, was suffering from severe malaria.[97]

October/November 2010: Following a crackdown on Christians in the Southern Zone ordered by the region's governor, security officials rounded up Christians living in the cities of Mendefera, Dekemharre and Dibarwa. Most of those detained belong to the Full Gospel Church, an Evangelical church that was banned in 2002. 11 members of the Church remained in detention several days after the arrests in late October.[98]

India

Population	Religions	Christian Pop.
1.15 billion	Hindu 80% Muslim 14% Christian 2% Seikh 2%, Other 2%	22 million

Churches across India continue to be overshadowed by the memory of the severe anti-Christian violence that broke out in 2007 and 2008 in Orissa state's Kandhamal district. There, 70 churches and other Christian institutions were attacked and 600 homes were destroyed when extremists interrupted Christmas preparations in late 2007. Far worse was to follow in August 2008, when Hindu monk and political leader Swami Laxmanananda Saraswati was assassinated. The Vishwa Hindu Parishad (VHP) movement, of which the Swami was a high-ranking member, falsely accused Christians in Kandhamal of carrying out the killing. It sparked a campaign of anti-Christian violence resulting in the torching of 4,640 houses, 252 churches and 13 educational institutions. Up to 500 people may have died in the violence that continued for several weeks. 54,000 were made homeless, seeking shelter in hastily-prepared displacement camps.[99] More than two years later, Archbishop Raphael Cheenath of Cuttack-Bhubaneswar was reporting that "large numbers" of people were still living in makeshift shelters in the camps.[100] Amid threats of renewed violence and forced conversions, many Christians were too afraid to return home.

Responsibility for the 2007/08 atrocities and much of the subsequent violence against Christians lies with Hindutva groups and other extremist political parties. Hindutva is a right-wing form of Hindu nationalism, which – broadly speaking – regards India as a Hindu country which should not tolerate other religions or cultures. The impact of Hindutva violence and intimidation, centred on Orissa, sent shockwaves throughout the country, not least because similar violence took place in a number of very disparate parts of the country. More than a year later, at the end of 2009, Dr Dominic Emmanuel, spokesperson for Delhi Catholic Archdiocese, was still reporting: "The trend of attacks on the Christian community by right-wing Hindu groups goes unabated. Overall, the Christian community still feels insecure."[101] Frequently attacks on Christians are associated with the Bharatiya Janata Party (BJP) gaining political power.

In 2009 Ajay Maken, Minister of Internal Affairs, presented a report to the

Rajya Sabha, the Indian parliament's upper house, indicating that religious-based violence had risen steeply over the past five years. It described more than 3,800 attacks by extremists, with numbers of reported attacks rising from 677 in 2004 to 943 in 2008. The country has seen an average of two attacks every day. The states named as having the highest number of reported incidents were Maharashtra (681), Madhya Pradesh (654) and Uttar Pradesh (613). The report came during the year of India's general elections, in which extremist party candidates made inflammatory anti-Christian speeches, some of which were seen as inciting hatred and violence.

After the 2008 violence, religious groups worked with politicians to tackle attacks on Christians and minorities. Leaders of many faith groups made public efforts to show respect for other religious communities by celebrating their holidays and attending social events such as weddings. Among those protesting against the maltreatment of Christians were Muslim leaders. This was especially significant in a country whose 200 million-strong Muslims represent the world's second largest Islamic community.[102]

Although anti-Christian attacks fell between 2008 and 2010,[103] a high number of isolated incidents of violence continued to be reported. Many of these assaults occurred in the context of false accusations of forced conversion. Of India's 28 states, five have 'anti-conversion' laws, which impose heavy fines and jail sentences for those 'forcing' others to change their religion. The 'anti-conversion' laws are imposed in the north-central states of Madhya Pradesh and Chhattisgarh, Orissa in the east, Gujarat in the west and Himachal Pradesh in the north. Hindu hardliners routinely engineer the arrest of Christians on charges of 'forcible conversion'. In particular, attacks against small evangelical churches appeared to be on the rise, particularly in Karnataka in southern India. Evangelical Christians' highly assertive, and sometimes culturally insensitive, evangelistic approach has been described as provocative to local Hindu communities. Meantime, reports emerged of extremists carrying out large-scale 're-conversions' of thousands of Christians to Hinduism. When, in December 2009, Hindus 'reconverted' 1,747 people in Gujarat, a state with 'anti-conversion' laws, the US State Department commented: "It is unknown whether the organisers sought prior permission from the district authorities."[104]

The Dalit question continues to be important, as many Dalits have converted to Christianity. Dalits – traditionally referred to as 'Untouchables' – are perceived as being at the bottom of the rigid caste system and experience discrimination because of this. Hence, the distinction between religion and social status is blurred. In March 2010 several bishops were detained in Tamil Nadu state after police halted a march protesting against the discrimination suffered by Dalit Christians.

February 2009: Fears about the fate awaiting Christians returning from displacement camps were hightened, after the body of 45-year-old Hrudyananda Nayak was discovered in Orissa's Kandhamal district. Mr Nayak was stopped by a group of Hindu extremists the previous evening.[105]

July 2009: Bishop Jose Mukala reported an upsurge in attacks and threats against Catholics in Kohima by some Baptist and Evangelical communities. Christian fundamentalists destroyed a Catholic church. Bishop Mukala stressed that the anti-Catholic activity did not originate with religious leaders. He said: "The opposition does not come from Protestant pastors, but from village leaders. They say there should be one state, one tribe and one religion."[106]

December 2009: A church was burnt during the night in the Karimnagar district of Andhra Pradesh state. Members of Hindutva groups Rashtriya Swayam Sevaks (RSS) and BJP poured petrol on Jesus Lights Manna Church, setting it on fire. Police officials arrested two men in connection with the offence.[107]

January 2010: Hindu radicals disrupted the Heavens Glory Ministries house church's Sunday service in Jalliguda, Hyderabad City, Andhra Pradesh state. Approximately 50 members from RSS and BJP disrupted the meeting at around 9am. Accusing Pastor Johnson of forcible conversion, the extremists beat him and any member of the congregation who tried to help him. Services were not held on the following two Sundays for fear of further attacks.[108]

January 2010: Two Catholic churches were desecrated and damaged in Karnataka. The first incident occurred after midnight in the village of Thernamakki in Karwar diocese. Unidentified people vandalised the grotto of the local church and broke its windows. There was further violence in

Inkal village, Mysore diocese, where vandals desecrated the statue of St Mary in the compound attached to Holy Family Church. Bishop Derek Fernandes of Karwar believed the attack was the work of Hindu activists. The Holy Family Church was previously attacked in February 2002, when 70 armed Hindutva activists attacked women and children during Mass.[109]

January 2010: About 50 Hindu extremists accused Rev Satyam Yellasiri of the Good Shepherd Community Church of forced conversion and tried to make him eat food offered to Hindu idols in Secunderabad, Andhra Pradesh state. When he refused, he was beaten.[110]

February 2010: In Thagadur village, Kodagu district of Karnataka, 11 Christians – including four women – were dragged from their homes to the police station, where officers were asked to arrest them on charges of forced conversion.[111]

February 2010: Extremists attempted to rape a refugee at Mondakai displacement camp in Phulbani, Kandhamal. An unidentified man followed Afasari Nayak as she went to bathe in a river near the camp. Nayak shouted for help as the man started attacking her, and people rushed to her aid. At about 7pm the suspect returned to the camp with four others and threatened to hurt the Christians if they filed a complaint, adding that the refugees should not return to their homes unless they converted to Hinduism.[112]

February 2010: Police arrested 11 Christians in Badimunda, Orissa state, after Hindu extremists accused them of assault. Hindu extremists shouted insults at two Christians and threatened to harm them unless they stopped worshipping Jesus. When the two Christians refused, the extremists began beating them. The two Christians managed to escape further attack after other people arrived on the scene. At about 7.30pm the following day, five extremists forcibly entered the house of Christian Dibyakand Nayak. In doing so, one of the extremists hurt his own forehead and this enraged the other extremists, who started beating Nayak. They damaged household goods before dragging him to the police station. Police arrested 11 Christians for allegedly using dangerous weapons and performing obscene acts and songs.[113]

February 2010: In Batala, Punjab state, some Christians were beaten and two churches were vandalised after a protest over a picture of Christ holding a cigarette and a beer can. The picture was part of a poster for the upcoming Ram Naumi Hindu festival. The poster contained images of other religious deities without any satirical additions. The poster is thought to be linked to Hindus who set fire to two churches and beat a Church of North India minister and a Salvation Army officer.[114]

March 2010: An independent investigation by Justice Michael Saldanha, a former judge of the Karnataka High Court, revealed that Christians in Karnataka state had faced more than 1,000 attacks in 500 days.[115]

March 2010: A mob of around 150 people, led by Hindutva politicians and Bajrang Dal – the VHP's youth movement – interrupted the funeral of a 50-year-old Christian. As Rev Sunder Raj was about to begin the service at St Thomas Church in Gijahalli, Karnataka state, the mob pulled the coffin apart and dragged the body out of the church. They said his burial would contaminate Indian soil and should be taken to Rome or the USA.[116]

April 2010: Amit Gilbert, a 25-year-old Christian, drowned in a well when fleeing from Hindu radicals who attacked a prayer meeting in the village of Saliya, Madhya Pradesh state. The man jumped inside the well when trying to escape his attackers. Three others at the prayer meeting were wounded.[117]

April 2010: Christians in Bhopal held a protest march demanding protection from the ruling BJP government. Leading the march, Archbishop Leo Cornelio of Bhopal criticised the BJP for making religious minorities victims of a "sustained malicious campaign". The archbishop said the government had created a sense of insecurity among Christians.[118]

August 2010: A Catholic school in Madhya Pradesh state was attacked. Furniture, computers and windows were destroyed but, with the attack taking place before the day's classes, no one was hurt.[119]

August 2010: Prahlad Remani, a BJP politician and a member of the Karnataka legislature, allegedly called for voters to "weed out Christians" from society. His comments were reportedly made at a local celebration marking Indian Independence Day (15th August). The following day, Christians demonstrated in front of local government offices.[120]

September 2010: US Pastor Terry Jones's proposed *Qur'an* burning in protest at the planned Islamic Centre near the site of the Twin Towers in New York sparked an angry response in Jammu and Kashmir state. The

Church of North India's Tyndale Biscoe School, whose students were all Muslim, was burnt down. Following a local mosque's call for a protest, a crowd of up to 20,000 marched to the school and set fire to it. Principal Pravez Samuel Kaul said: "The whole three-storey structure with 26 classrooms, library, and computer labs burnt down to the ground. Ironically, our library had various copies of the *Qur'an*." The following day a mob set fire to the Catholic Church's Good Shepherd School in Pulwama, but police intervened, minimising damage to the buildings. Two Protestant schools in Pooch Jammu were also attacked, Christ School and Christ Mohalla School. The resulting clashes between police and thousands of demonstrators left at least 17 dead and 80 wounded. Shortly after, thousands of protesters assembled close to a Christian school in Mendhar. Police used tear gas as protesters tried to enter the school. They used live ammunition when they refused to disperse. At least three protesters were killed and 30 were wounded.[121]

September 2010: Representatives of the Church of South India, Syrian Catholic Church, Orthodox Churches and the Syro-Malabar Congregation of the Carmelites of Mary Immaculate, gathered in Kozhikode, Kerala state for the first meeting of the Christian Democratic Union. The group was formed after the hand of a Christian teacher was slashed. The group expressed concern over Christians being forced to convert to another religion and sent to Kashmir to fight. They also said Christians in the state had declined from 30 percent in 1950 to less than 20 percent in 2010.[122]

November 2010: Around 250 Hindutva extremists stormed the villages of Peliguda, Kenduguda and Telarai near the town of Malkangiri, Orissa State. The militants broke into Christian homes and assaulted Christians. The attacks were filmed by journalists from ETV 2, an Indian television station. Villagers claimed they were attacked for refusing to contribute to the Hindu Druga Puja festival.[123]

December 2010: Hindutva radicals attacked Protestant Christians in Karnataka State. In Bangalore, the state capital, extremists threatened 50 worshippers at Gipsy Prayer Hall during a Sunday service. A group of 40 people surrounded the Pentecostal Church of Jyothinagar and threw stones at the building. In Shimoga district, radicals beat up and dragged four Christians out of two churches, before having them arrested on charges of proselytism.[124]

Profile: Sister Meena from Orissa, India

The rape of Sister Meena Barwa close to the pastoral centre in India where she worked was to become a potent symbol of an outbreak of anti-Christian persecution scarcely paralleled in modern times.

The largely rural community of Kandhamal district in eastern India's Orissa state was torn apart by a series of attacks, which by the turn of 2009 had left more than 50,000 people displaced and more than 5,500 homes destroyed.

In the violence that affected 300 villages, up to 500 people died, including a priest, Fr Bernard Digal. 290 churches and chapels were desecrated. Few events of those terrible days did more to underline the sheer cruelty of the attacks than revelations about what happened to Sr Meena.

In reports given by those present at the time, including an emotional press conference given by Sr Meena herself, it is possible to piece together the events as they unfolded that fateful day.

At around 4.30 on the afternoon of August 24th 2008 a large noisy crowd gathered at the gate of Divyajyoti Pastoral Centre, Konjamendi. Warned by reports of mob violence spreading across Kandhamal, staff at the centre reacted quickly when the mob began assembling outside the gates.

Sister Meena, 29, who worked at the centre, was among a group of staff members including the director, Fr Thomas Chellan, who slipped out of the back door.

By the time the mob had entered, Sr Meena, Fr Chellan and the others had escaped to the relative safety of the surrounding forest.

Later that same evening, a local Hindu – Prahallad Pradhan – and his wife, Chanchala, gave them shelter in their home.

But any relief they might have felt was short-lived. Suddenly a mob of up to 50 people armed with lathes, spades, crowbars, iron rods and sickles turned up outside Prahallad Pradhan's home and burst into the building.

In a press conference held two months later amid a storm of local media interest, Sr Meena gave a statement saying: "One of the men entered the room where I was staying in that house, caught my hair and pulled me out."

But before the axe could be wielded against her, the attackers gave into requests from others in the mob to take her outside.

Out in the road, she saw Fr Chellan being beaten. The two of them were taken to the nearby Jana Vikas Catholic social action centre. The building had been set ablaze and was still smouldering.

"The [attackers] threw me on the veranda [of Jana Vikas] on the way to the dining room which was full of ashes and broken glass pieces."

They tore at her clothes and under-garments. Restraining her by standing on her hands, she was raped in full view of the crowd. No sooner was it over when another man grabbed her. He was "attempting to rape" her when a man in the crowd told him to stop.

Momentarily escaping her attackers' clutches she hid under the nearby staircase. The mob soon caught up with her. She later recalled: "The crowd was shouting: 'Where is that Sister? Come, let us rape her; at least 100 people should rape her.'"

Soon she was discovered and she was dragged outside again. There, she saw Fr Chellan kneeling down, being beaten. She could hear voices among the mob calling for the two of them to be set on fire. Some of the crowd were searching for a rope to tie them together.

But again, they were spared. Instead, virtually naked, the two were forced to walk a third of a mile (5 km), during which time she recalled people slapping her on the face and head and hitting her on the back with a stick.

Arriving in a market place, Sr Meena at last caught sight of the police. She recalled seeing up to a dozen officers. She quickly approached them. "I asked them to protect me but they did not move."

Sr Meena said that the police had a "very friendly" conversation with one of her assailants.

Only later was she taken into police custody but was initially advised against filing a complaint against her attackers. "They tried their best so that I would not register an FIR [First Incident Report – equivalent to a statement to the police] and not make complaints against the police. The police did not take down my statement which I narrated in detail and they abandoned me half of the way [through]."

Shortly after, two doctors examined Sr Meena but it is alleged that police delayed 38 days before collecting the medical report confirming that she was raped. The hospital is directly opposite the police station.

In March 2010 a trial in Cuttack was underway against those accused of the 2008 anti-Christian attacks in Kandhamal against Christians including Sister Meena. In November 2010 she identified the fifth of a possible 10 people who attacked her.[125]

Meantime, her uncle, Bishop John Barwa, of Rourkela, Orissa, paid tribute to his niece, describing how in the months and years since her attack she has rebuilt her life, continuing her academic studies and taking her final vows as a religious Sister.

He said: "She is five times more courageous than me. We come from a very rural background. God has chosen one of our family members – Sister Meena – as an instrument of his courage and witness."

"With regards the identification of the culprits, she said that it is God who enlightens her and the Holy Spirit that gives her the strength to face them again. The last time we were together before such a moment, we held a beautiful Eucharistic celebration together with her superior. We celebrated for over three hours in prayer, with the Word of God, in Eucharistic healing. A gift of grace and peace for all of us."[126]

Indonesia

Population	Religions	Christian Population
238 million	Muslim 79% Christian 12% Local religions 2.5% Other 6.5%	28.5 million

Indonesia's President, Susilo Bambang Yudhoyono, has taken steps to tackle religious intolerance and the rise of militant extremism, especially in historically sensitive regions such as Ambon and Central Sulawesi. However, attacks and acts of intimidation against religious minorities have continued.

Indonesia has seen a rise in Islamic fundamentalism since early 2009. Human rights and religious freedom organisations reported many acts of violence, ranging from church buildings burnt to the ground, to authorities cancelling Easter services at very short notice under pressure from local fundamentalists. On the eve of national and regional elections on 9th April 2009, Christians expressed concern over growing support for Islamist parties, including the Partai Bulan Bintang and Partai Keadilan Sejahtera, both of which want to impose *Shari'a* law.

Although Aceh is the only province completely governed by *Shari'a*, more than 50 regencies (in 16 of the country's 32 provinces) have passed *Shari'a* inspired legislation. These laws vary widely. In Padang, West Sumatra, both Muslim and non-Muslim women must wear headscarves, while in Tangerang lone women found "loitering" on the street after 10pm may be arrested and charged with prostitution. Other laws include stipulations for Qur'anic literacy among schoolchildren.[127]

Some national and provincial laws, such as those on blasphemy and building permits, have been used against minorities. In April 2010 the Constitutional Court rejected a challenge seeking to repeal the blasphemy law. The Wahid Institute – a Muslim research centre focusing on interfaith issues – reported that in 2009 there were 35 cases of government violations of religious freedom (including 28 against Christians) and 93 instances of local intolerance of Christian communities.[128]

Christian groups claimed that religious workers experienced problems obtaining or extending visas and added that the necessary criteria were far less onerous for other categories including foreigners entering the country.

July 2009: Muslim groups stopped the construction of a home for disabled children in Junrejo, on the outskirts of Batu in Malang, East Java, claiming it might be used for evangelisation. Sister Chatarina Sulasti of the Institut Sekulir Alma, a secular women's institution supporting the project, rejected all allegations of proselytising.

October 2009: Two churches in Jakarta received bomb threats. In north Bekasi, in the Jakarta metropolitan area, Jeffry Lalamentik, a church leader at Bethel Indonesia congregation, received a bomb threat. The caller said: "Your church will be bombed during morning worship."[129]

October 2009: Up to 1,000 students from Arastamar Evangelical Theological Seminary resisted efforts to evict them from the former municipal building in West Jakarta which they had been using since Muslim protestors drove them from their campus in 2008. A banner at their original building read: "If you dare to return, we will wipe you out". The students claimed new facilities offered by the Jakarta Provincial Government were in a terrible condition.[130]

January 2010: Local governments ordered the closure of two churches on Java island – the Christian Baptist Church in Sepatan, Tangerang district, Banten Province and the Huria Christian Protestant Batak Church in Pondok Timur, near Bekasi in West Java. Reports suggest the closures are linked to pressure from militant Islamic groups. The problem started after Islamic groups organised demonstrations against the church in Sepatan. On 19th December 2009, 30 people demonstrated during a children's Christmas celebration. A week later a large crowd from the Islamic Defenders' Front arrived and demanded that worship cease. Two days later the pastor received a letter from local police ordering that services stop on the grounds that they violated local government regulations.[131]

January 2010: Up to 1,000 Muslims set fire to a Protestant church under construction in Sibuhuan in the province of North Sumatra. The same day Padanglawas Pentecostal Church was also set on fire.[132]

February 2010: Hundreds of Muslims gathered to call for the closure of Galilea Protestant Church in the Galaxy area of Bekasi City, West Java. Taking part were demonstrators from 16 Islamic organisations, including the Islamic Defenders Front. Most protestors came from outside the Galaxy area. Rev M. Tetelepta said the church was officially approved for religious purposes and had also been recognised in this capacity by local residents.[133]

March 2010: Two churches had building permits cancelled following protests by Muslim groups. Fr Peter Kurniawan Subagyo of Santa Maria Immaculata in Citra Garden, West Jakarta, said he had received a permit for a new church after the 20,000-strong congregation outgrew their existing building. A few weeks after construction work got underway, Islamic groups began demonstrations. Officials subsequently cancelled the permit.[134]

May 2010: A blasphemous website posting led members of the Islamic Defenders Front to attack the St Bellarminus School in Bekasi district, West Java. The violence came in response to an anonymous posting on a blog, allegedly run by the school, containing offensive statements about Islam. It was accompanied by a photograph of the *Qur'an* in a toilet. Sister Ignatio Nudek from St Bellarminus' said: "This school does not have such a blog. We never disgrace other religions. In fact we have Muslim students at the school."[135]

August 2010: As around 20 members of the Batak Christian Protestant Filadelfia Church in Bekasi arrived for Sunday worship, members of the Islamic People's Forum and the Islamic Defenders Front broke through a police cordon and ordered them to leave. Up to 700 protestors took part in the attack on the 1,500-strong congregation.[136]

September 2010: 300 Christians held a protest march to the Indonesian National Police headquarters in Jakarta following attacks on two Protestant clerics in Bekasi, West Java. Rev Luspida Simanjuntak and her assistant pastor Hasean Lumbantoruan Sihombing of the Batak Society Christian Church were attacked while on their way to Sunday service. Sihombing was stabbed in the stomach while Simanjuntak suffered concussion after being hit on the head with a plank.[137]

November 2010: Addressing 500 religious and laypeople at the Third Grand Synod of the Indonesian Catholic Church, Bogor, West Java, Suryadharma Ali, minister of Religious Affairs, described the Catholic Church as a key partner in achieving progress in education. He said religions play a role in finding solutions to violence, terrorism and response to natural disasters.[138]

Iran

Population	Religions	Christian Population
72 million	Muslim 98.5% Other 1.5%	15,000

The world's leading *Shia* Muslim country, Iran remains firmly in the grip of a ruling elite whose concept of religious tolerance inevitably places minority groups – including Sunni Muslims – at a distinct disadvantage. But Christians are especially at risk from institutionalised violence and discrimination. According to human rights observers, the problems have been exacerbated by continuing political tension. Normally concealed from the rest of the world, the country's instability became international headline news in summer 2009 with the widespread demonstrations and turmoil following the controversial re-election of arch-conservative President Mahmoud Ahmadinejad. The clampdown on opponents and other dissidents was of grave concern to the country's Christians who have been falsely accused of pro-Western sympathies at a time of intense anti-US sentiment.[139]

Among religious minorities, only three are recognised by the state, Christians, Jews and Zoroastrians. However, their legal status is precarious, a problem that Pope Benedict XVI addressed in a November 2010 letter to President Ahmadinejad. Members of recognised religious minorities live as *dhimmis*, second-class citizens. They cannot spread their beliefs or bear witness to them outside their communities or places of worship. One of the main problems is translating religious texts into the native language of Farsi. The religious authorities in Iran have expressed concerned about non-Islamic texts becoming available in the main language used in the country. There have been reports of Church centres being closed after the authorities discovered that religious texts were being translated into Farsi.

The prohibition on "apostasy" – renouncing Islam – is very firmly enforced both by the apostate's family and the government. In September 2008, the Iranian parliament approved a new Penal Code which imposed the death penalty for the crime of apostasy. This law, however, was waiting to be studied in depth by a parliamentary commission. However in 2009 the Parliamentary Commission for Law and Judgement decided to exclude the amendment which would have carried the death penalty for apostasy.

Sensational and exaggerated reports about mass conversions from Islam have resulted in arrests among the Christian communities. According to some religious-rights organisations, the problem is exacerbated by reports filtering back to Iran of 'well-intentioned' Christian leaders who publicised inflated figures about new converts. One agency reported that in any given year many thousands were converting to Christianity. The government, the report said, considered such a high apostasy rate to be a threat to its rule and had responded by attacking churches.

The ongoing – and in many respects intensifying – anti-Christian climate explains the haemorrhaging number of Christians since the 1979 Iranian Revolution led by Ayatollah Khomeini. According to reports released in November 2010, the number of Assyrian (native) Christians had dwindled from about 100,000 in the mid-1970s to barely 15,000. The impact of this is all the more devastating when in the same period the overall population swelled from 38 million to 72 million.[140]

January 2009: Three members of the Church of the Assemblies of God were arrested in the capital, Teheran: Jamal Ghalishorani, aged 49, and his wife Nadereh Jamali – both of whom had converted from Islam, 30 and 15 years earlier respectively – and Armenian Christian, Hamik Khachikian. While their church had been officially registered, all three had held Bible studies in their private homes. At the beginning of February they were released on bail.

March 2009: Two Christian converts from Islam – Maryam Rostampour, aged 27, and Marzieh Amirizadeh Esmaeilabad, 30 – were arrested and charged with "acting against the security of the state". They were accused of "having attended illegal assemblies" in Teheran. They were both active in distributing Bibles in their churches. They appeared in an Islamic Court in Teheran before being taken to prison. They were denied medical care even though both women were suffering from infections and fever. In August 2009 they appeared before a judge. They were told they faced a long jail term if they did not renounce their apostasy and return to Islam. Following international pressure they were released in November 2009 and were finally acquitted of all charges in May 2010. They have since left the country.

March 2009: An Islamic Court in Shiraz sentenced three Christian converts – Seyed Allaedin Hussein, Homayoon Shokouhi and Seyed Amir Hussein Bob-Annari – to an eight month suspended sentence and five years on probation. They were charged with "cooperating with anti-government movements" – a reference to Christian TV stations. They were forbidden from contacting one another and participating in Christian activities including prayer services and evangelisation work. The judge threatened to enforce the sentence and have them tried for apostasy if all three did not strictly observe these instructions.

May 2009: 62-year-old pensioner Abdul Zahra Vashahi was arrested in the city of Bandar Mahshar. He was detained in an attempt to stop the activities of his son, 30-year-old John Reza Vashahi, a convert to Christianity who has been living in the UK since 2003. In 2008 John Vashahi founded the Iranian Minorities Human Rights Organization. He is also the author of a blog entitled "Jesus for Arabs." His father, who is a Muslim, was released after being held and interrogated for six days.[141]

July 2009: Police raided a meeting of Christians – all converts from Islam – in Fashan (north of Teheran). All 24 Christians at the meeting were arrested and devotional objects and other materials were seized. 17 of those arrested were released the following day. Two days earlier, another eight Christians from the same group were arrested in Rasht. According to local Christians, the wave of arrests intensified after the disputed presidential elections. The faithful were arrested for alleged collusion with "foreign powers" which were supposedly behind the demonstrations criticising the leadership.

July 2009: Several satellite channels, including Christian broadcaster SAT-7, had their signals into Iran blocked by the government. After June's presidential elections the government restricted mobile phone and satellite in order to stop citizens organising demonstrations against President Mahmoud Ahmadinejad.[142]

December 2009: Security officers with an arrest warrant from the Mashhad Revolutionary Court entered the home of Christian Hamideh Najafi in Mashhad. After searching her home and confiscating personal belongings, including books and CDs, police took her away. Najafi was sentenced to three months under house arrest. The court further ordered that her daughter, who suffers from a kidney condition, be placed in foster care. However, because of the seriousness of the girl's illness, she was left in her parents' custody – providing they abandon the Christian faith and stop speaking publicly about it.[143]

January 2010: Over the previous few months, at least 14 Christians were jailed for more than two weeks and all were denied legal advice. Among those held at Evin prison were 12 people who had celebrated Christmas in a house 12 miles (19 km) south-east of Teheran.[144]

February 2010: The Rev Wilson Issavi, leader of the Assyrian Evangelical Church, was arrested by local agents of state security while visiting an old friend in Shahin Shahr, Isfahan. He was taken to an undisclosed location. In January local security agents had closed down his church. His wife reported that he appeared to have been tortured while in prison. He was released on bail in April.[145]

October 2010: The US Commission on International Religious Freedom urged President Obama to call on Iran to release Youcef Nadarkhani, a Christian minister facing the death sentence. He had been arrested for apostasy and for questioning the dominant role of Islamic instruction at his children's school. In October 2009 Mr Nadarkhani's wife, Fatemeh Passandideh, was released after four months in prison on charges of apostasy.[146]

November 2010: In a letter to President Mahmoud Ahmadinejad, Pope Benedict XVI called for talks on the status of the Catholic Church in Iran. His concerns centre on the regime's failure to grant official status to the Conference of Iranian Bishops. The letter, which was made public by the Vatican press office, was a reply to a missive from President Ahmadinejad the previous month in which the Iranian leader called for stronger bilateral relations with the Vatican to fight secularisation. In his reply, the Pope also drew attention to the difficult conditions faced by Christian minorities in the Middle East. He wrote: "In some countries these communities face difficult circumstances, discrimination and even violence and they lack the freedom to live and publicly profess their faith." He said religious people could play a key role in spreading peace.[147]

December 2010/January 2011: Shortly after Christmas authorities started arresting Christians from 'house churches'. About 70 Christians were arrested.[148]

Iraq

Population	Religions	Christian Population
30 million	Shia Muslim: 60% Sunni Muslim 37% Others 3%	200,000

In Iraq the very survival of one of the world's oldest Christian communities now hangs in the balance. Continuing attacks against the faithful have prompted successive waves of emigration. According to UN reports in 2010, of the 1.6 million Iraqi refugees abroad, up to 40 percent were thought to be Christians.[149] According to some of the country's most senior bishops, over the past decade the number of Christians haemorrhaged from nearly 900,000 to perhaps fewer than 200,000, a rate of decline far steeper than official figures suggest. By 2011, some sources gave an even lower figure for the number of Christians left in Iraq. Nor does there seem any end in sight to the problem, with Christian emigration continuing unabated.

Catholic leaders said the number of Christians remaining in Baghdad by early 2011 would be a mere fraction of the 200,000 living there at the start of 2003. Even more Christians fled the city after the 31st October 2010 siege of Baghdad's Our Lady of Salvation Syrian Catholic Cathedral. The massacre of at least 52 people – the worst atrocity to befall Iraq's Christians in modern times – put the international spotlight on the plight of the country's frightened and bewildered faithful. It was now beyond doubt that Christians were the specific target of the attacks, and that the message extremists wanted to send out was that Christians should leave Iraq. Between 2003 and 2010 more than 2,000 Christians are thought to have been killed by violence, many targeted primarily because of their faith.[150] Church figures said recently that one bishop and six priests had been killed since 2002 and more than 30 churches attacked. After successive attacks against Christian churches, homes and businesses, many Christians had become desperate for a new beginning in a new country, preferably in the West. Pressure has been mounting for Western countries to provide asylum for Iraqi Christians, although many Catholic leaders called for the faithful to stay in the country if at all possible.

Christians were under threat not only in Baghdad but all over the country where attacks were taking place with varying degrees of severity. The northern city of Mosul was a focus for especially vicious violence. In

66

autumn 2008 a campaign of intimidation, including the assassination of more than a dozen Christians, sparked a mass exodus of more than 12,000 Christians from the city.[151] They were still reeling from the tragic loss of Archbishop Paulos Faraj Rahho of Mosul. The sick prelate was kidnapped outside his cathedral in Mosul at the end of February 2008 and died in captivity. Barely two weeks after he was taken into captivity, his body was dumped in the city in a shallow grave. A boost to morale came in January 2010, when Amil Nona was appointed as Mgr Rahho's successor as Archbishop of Mosul. Aged 42, he became reportedly the world's youngest Catholic archbishop.[152]

But youth and optimism would face an apparently insurmountable obstacle in the form of continuing attacks on churches and other Christian communities. In early 2010, a further wave of violence and intimidation forced more than 4,000 Christians to flee Mosul.[153] It soon emerged that safety could not be guaranteed even in the ancient Christian villages in the famous Nineveh Plains outside Mosul. Threats and occasional attacks in this, a principal heartland of Christianity in the region, made plain the scale of the threat against the faithful. Matters came to a head in May 2010, when a convoy of Christian buses travelling from Nineveh Christian villages to Mosul came under fire. In the ambush, 190 Christian youngsters received injuries, mostly to their faces.

The seemingly unrelenting intimidation and violence against Christians meant increasing numbers of faithful felt they had no option but to flee. The most immediate place of sanctuary has proved to be the Kurdish north of Iraq. However, continuing fears for their safety and acute poverty have forced vast numbers to travel abroad to neighbouring Syria, Jordan and Turkey. Many have been desperate to start a new life in the West. In Syria, Bishop Antoine Audo of Aleppo masterminded a programme of emergency aid for Iraqi Christian refugees, providing medical aid, shelter, food and community support. His relief work was among a number of refugee programmes supported by charities including Aid to the Church in Need.

Back in Iraq, the continuing attacks on people of all faiths – Sunni and Shiite Muslims especially – made clear that the Christians were not the only ones being targeted. However, their ever-dwindling numbers and their complete reliance on government security meant that the Christians' suffering was especially tragic. But amid all the suffering the stoic example of individual Christians told a very different story, one of faithful dedication in times of acute misery. On 3rd June 2007, Fr Ragheed Ganni was killed not far from his Holy Spirit Church in Mosul. The one survivor of the shoot-out, which also claimed the lives of three sub-deacons, later told how the gunmen condemned 35-year-old Fr Ragheed for not closing his church. The priest responded: "How could I close the house of God?" Moments later he was shot dead. Fr Ragheed's memory was an inspiration to many, especially other young clergy. A week after the 31st October 2010 massacre at Baghdad's Syrian Catholic Cathedral, two young priests came to serve the shell-shocked community, replacing two other young clergy shot dead on that fateful day.

The continued activity of extremist groups seemed to make clear that the campaign against insurgents had proved far from successful. When the 'Islamic State of Iraq', an organisation with links to al-Qaeda, took responsibility for attacks including the October 2010 Baghdad cathedral siege, it served as an indictment of the country's uncertain political situation nine months on from the inconclusive outcome of parliamentary elections. Amid international outrage about the country's apparently parlous security situation, the pressure was mounting on Jalal Talabani who, after months of political wrangling, emerged in late 2010 to start a second term as president.

April 2009: Three Christians were killed in the northern city of Kirkuk. Mrs Sudan Latif David, a woman just a year into her marriage, and her mother-in-law, Muna Banna David, were killed after armed men entered their home in the Domeez area of the city. At about the same time, elsewhere in the city, Basil Shaba was murdered in a similar attack. His brother, Thamir, and father, Yousif, who were with him at the time, were injured. Saying that Mr Shaba had "only recently got engaged", Archbishop Louis Sako of Kirkuk described the funeral: "People were crying. We are all so sad. We only hope that the blood of the martyrs will one day bring us peace and stability." Latest reports stated that nobody had yet been arrested in connection with the crimes.[154]

July 2009: At least four people were killed and 30 were injured in a series of bombings targeting five churches in Baghdad. The attacks on Sunday, 12th July began when two improvised explosives went off near two churches in the city's Wahda district and two others in Dora and Al Gadir, in eastern Baghdad. In the worst attack, a car bomb exploded just before nightfall at the Chaldean Church of the Virgin Mary in the city centre. The blast damaged the church and scorched cars in a nearby car park. A number of people – Muslims as well as Christians – were killed and injured. The attacks coincided with a roadside bomb in Nasiriya, southern Iraq, aimed at the US ambassador to Iraq. The ambassador, who was travelling in convoy at the time, escaped unharmed. Nobody claimed responsibility for the attacks.[155]

September 2009: Reports showed Christians had begun fleeing northern Iraq's Nineveh Plains, the site of ancient Christian villages. This region, outside Mosul city, had been thought to be one of the last safe places for Christians in Iraq. In an ACN interview, senior Iraqi priest Fr Bashar Warda said Christians in Nineveh had received verbal threats. Some were abducted. Reporting that up to 40 Christians were fleeing the region every month, Fr Warda said: "I am sad to say that the emigration of Christian families that we have seen in places like Mosul and Baghdad has now begun to affect the Nineveh area."[156] A few months later Archbishop Louis Sako of Kirkuk said that displaced Christians seeking sanctuary in the Kurdish region of northern Iraq were now "leaving the country for good". He said they were fed up with the region's lack of clean water, schools, jobs and healthcare. He added: "In years gone by, Christians left their houses and property and reached a secure area in the hope of being back soon." He continued: "Now six years have passed", adding that they had lost all hope of returning home.

January 2010: Following another attack on Christians in Baghdad, Latin Catholic Archbishop Jean Sleiman of Baghdad said: "Let us break the wall of silence that surrounds the killing of Christians in Iraq. Christians are killed in Mosul while the state does nothing. The forces of order serving in the places of the attacks and killings don't see, don't hear, don't speak."[157]

January 2010: Amil Nona was installed as the Archbishop of Mosul, becoming aged 42 the world's youngest Catholic archbishop. He replaced Archbishop Paulos Faraj Rahho, who died in captivity two years earlier, shortly after being kidnapped outside his cathedral. In a statement to ACN, the new archbishop described his mission as "providing hope and confidence to the Christians, making them aware of the presence of a father and a minister beside them in their present plight". He said that amid increasing terrorist attacks on Christians and widespread emigration of wealthier Christians, those left behind were clinging to their faith. He said: "The only thing that the faithful are still adhering to is the Church."[158] Barely three weeks later, Archbishop Nona warned of a fresh campaign to drive Mosul's remaining Christians out of the city, after four Christians were killed in separate attacks within one week. The archbishop spoke to ACN after the death of the fourth person, 20-year-old student teacher Wissam Georges. He said: "It is very difficult to live in this kind of situation. It is panic – panic always. The Christians don't know what will happen to them. They don't know if somebody is going to kill them."[159]

May 2010: One person died and nearly 190 were wounded – 24 seriously – when attackers ambushed a convoy of student buses entering Mosul, en route to the city's university. The attacks, which took place between two checkpoints on the edge of the city, caused glass from bus windows to spray all over the students sitting inside. Many of them had facial wounds – including severe eye injuries – and a number were taken to hospital in the Kurdish capital, Erbil, where their condition was described as serious but stable. Afterwards Catholic leaders met a delegation of 300 students from Mosul University who pleaded for action to improve security and bring the attackers to justice. Archbishop Louis Sako of Kirkuk told ACN: "When we saw the students, we were very moved. They were so very shocked and felt discouraged. Many were injured – with bandages on their faces and some over their eyes. There was crying and a lot of sadness. One student told us that it was a miracle so few people died."[160]

August 2010: Ali-al-Musawi, media spokesman for Iraq Prime Minister Nuri al-Maliki, said the government was doing everything possible to ensure security, but added that religious and ethnic minorities were especially vulnerable and needed more done to protect them. He gave his comments after the US Senate adopted a resolution earlier in August 2010 highlighting the "perilous status of religious minorities in Iraq" and called on the government to address abuses against them.[161]

October/November 2010: 58 people died and more than 70 were injured on 31st October when extremists carried out an attack during Sunday Mass at Our Lady of Deliverance Syrian Catholic Cathedral, Baghdad. The 'Islamic State of Iraq', an organisation with links to al-Qaeda, claimed responsibility for the attack. The terrorists entered the cathedral wearing suicide vests and holding automatic weapons. About 100 people were herded to the centre of the cathedral while a priest ushered 60 others into a small room at the back of the building. The attackers demanded the release of al-Qaeda prisoners including the widow of Abu Omar al-Baghdadi, the former head of the 'Islamic State of Iraq', killed in April, as well as Muslim girls allegedly detained in Egyptian monasteries. Inside the cathedral, the gunmen taunted their victims with anti-Christian rhetoric and threats to blow up the building. Iraqi and US military surrounded the cathedral, resulting in a siege which climaxed with more violence. Two young priests were killed, Fathers Wasim Sabieh, aged 27, and Thaier Saad Abdal. A third priest, Fr Raphaele Quotani, 75, was taken to hospital with stomach wounds. Afterwards Benedict XVI said he was "praying for the victims of this absurd violence, which is even more ferocious as it struck defenceless people, gathered in the house of God, a house of love and reconciliation". A week later, three people died and 26 were injured in attacks on the homes of Christians in Baghdad. Again, the 'Islamic State of Iraq' claimed responsibility. Reports said that among those targeted was the family of a victim of the attacks in the cathedral the previous week. They were able to identify the family by funeral signs outside their home.[162]

November 2010: Within two weeks of the attack on Baghdad's Syrian Catholic cathedral, nearly 100 Christians had fled to the Iraqi city of Sulaimaniya. Many others had sought sanctuary elsewhere. Christians were not reassured by the arrest of 12 people in connection with the attack. Christians arriving in Sulaimaniya, as well as those in Baghdad and Mosul, denounced the arrests, saying they were principally intended to restore confidence among countries in the West.[163]

December 2010: Elderly Christian couple, Hikmat and Samira Sammak were stabbed to death in their house in the Baladiyat neighbourhood of Baghdad, on the evening of 5th December. Having moved to Ainkawa-Erbil in the north they had returned to finalise the sale of their old home.[164]

December 2010/January 2011: Two people died and a dozen others were wounded over Christmas when bombs were placed outside Christian homes in Baghdad. Archbishop Louis Sako of Kirkuk wrote: "For us Christians of Iraq, martyrdom is the charism of our church, in its 2,000-year history. We are aware that bearing witness to Christ can mean martyrdom."[165]

71

Profile: Archbishop Amil Nona of Mosul, Iraq

"It is panic – panic always. The Christians don't know what will happen to them. It's the same everywhere: in the office, at school and even at home. They don't know if somebody is going to kill them."

In an interview with Aid to the Church in Need, Archbishop Amil Nona is only too aware that his diocese of Mosul has suffered some of the worst persecution to befall the Church in a generation. Formerly an ancient centre of Christianity serving the entire region, Mosul – known in the Bible as Nineveh – still counted 25-30,000 faithful in 2003. But now, after years of violence which has targeted the Church in particular, Archbishop Amil estimates that only 5,000 remain or perhaps less. The very survival of one of the world's oldest Christian communities is at stake.

The flashpoints have been unrelenting but amid the near constant reports of murders, kidnappings and acts of intimidation – many targeting Christians – three stand out. In February 2008, Archbishop Paulos Faraj Rahho – Archbishop Amil's predecessor – was kidnapped outside his own cathedral. Already sick, he died in captivity and two weeks later his body was discovered in a shallow grave not far from the city centre. It underlined the gravity of a crisis that had already claimed the life of Mosul's Fr Ragheed Ganni aged just 35. After celebrating Mass one Sunday morning in June 2007, Fr Ragheed's car was ambushed and he was shot at point blank range. His killers pulled the trigger after he once again refused to close his church. The siege of the Syrian Catholic Cathedral in Baghdad on 31st October 2010 which left more than 50 dead, sent shockwaves across the country. This and another spate of killings in both Mosul and Baghdad caused a fresh exodus of faithful.

Against this bloody backdrop, Amil Nona leads his people as Archbishop of Mosul. At the time of his ordination to the episcopate in January 2010 he was, at 42, one of the world's youngest Catholic bishops. He knows he will need all the energy and enthusiasm of youth for the testing years ahead. But he takes up the heavy burden of responsibility knowing that his formative years earned him many friends – not just among the Christian faithful – but countless others besides. Many such friends date back to his earliest years. Amil and his 10 siblings are the sons and daughters of a popular bus driver in Alqosh, the staunchly Christian town outside Mosul in the Nineveh plains. Amil's father, who still lives in Alqosh, was a stalwart figure in a town which came under a very strict embargo during the 1970s and 1980s.

The people's suffering was what first stirred thoughts of priesthood in the mind of young Amil. He said: "I knew I wanted to serve others, to help them to know the truth and to derive hope from the truth." After training at St Peter's Seminary, then based in the Dora district of Baghdad, Amil was ordained priest in January 1991. The ceremony roughly coincided with the start of the first Gulf War. A brilliant student, he did further studies at the Lateran University, emerging with a PhD in anthropology and theology. As a parish priest back home in Alqosh, his commitment to youth catechesis led him to establish the 'theological cycle' which attracted 200 youngsters who took part in a weekly programme running for three years.

Despite all the training and pastoral experience, Amil Nona's appointment as Archbishop of Mosul could only have come as an enormous shock to him. Priest friends and others report that he is determined to remain a simple shepherd, putting the needs of others before himself. The archbishop's security is a major preoccupation – but not for him. A close friend from seminary days told ACN: "It is not the main issue for him. He has made his choice in life and he keeps his safety in the hands of God." In any case, a large security presence protecting the archbishop would only attract the attention of would-be assassins.

The archbishop admitted to fears for his safety but added: "I am more afraid that this ancient Christian community, here in Mosul, will evaporate – disappear for ever." It is not an over-statement. Barely a month after becoming Archbishop, a spate of murders, clearly targeting Christians, sparked an exodus of faithful mostly to the nearby Nineveh plains, the second such mass movement in barely 18 months. Sources close to the archbishop say his presence – his refusal to leave Mosul – was a key reason persuading many – if not all – to return.

Describing his mission, he said: "What I want to do is to serve, to give the people who are suffering a sense of hope, a reason for believing that a better future is possible. This can be achieved through good planning based on a realistic assessment of our difficult circumstances." Youth catechesis remains a key priority. In the summer of 2010, senior staff from St Peter's Seminary, now based in Ankawa, outside Erbil, the capital of Kurdistan, northern Iraq, said that four young men from Mosul were about to begin training for the priesthood. "They are receiving personal guidance and support from Archbishop Amil," said the seminary rector. "Archbishop Amil thinks this is very important." Given the security constraints, Archbishop Amil said one of the biggest problems is keeping in contact with the priests, Sisters and lay communities in his diocese. "This is very hard," he said, "because we need each other's support, especially at this time."

But in spite of all the trials and tribulations, Amil Nona professes a faith that is rock solid. He said: "We have huge problems, nobody can deny that. But my faith is very strong and I want to do everything I can – with God's help – to inspire the people, to encourage them not to lose hope and to lead them in times of darkness to better days."

Israel and Palestine

	Israel	Palestine
Population	7 million	4 million
Major religions	Judaism Islam	Islam
Christian population	150,000	

Growing concerns about the long-term survival of Christianity in the land of Christ's birth attracted international attention when Pope Benedict XVI visited the region in May 2009. To coincide with the papal pilgrimage, Archbishop Fouad Twal, the Latin Patriarch of Jerusalem, issued a pastoral letter setting out the scale of Christianity's decline across the region. In the letter, he gave statistics showing that Palestinian Christians in Jerusalem have declined from 53 percent in 1922 to less than two percent today. If trends continued, he added, today's figure of 10,000 could halve within a decade. Similarly, he reported that Christians in Bethlehem declined from 85 percent in 1948 to 12 percent in 2009.[166]

A key reason given for Christian emigration is a deepening climate of discrimination affecting Christians and other minorities. Four months on from the Pope's Holy Land visit, Patriarch Twal said that, in spite of the papal trip, the oppressive treatment of minorities – including Christians – had not improved. Speaking at an Aid to the Church in Need event in London, Patriarch Twal said: "Discrimination, always present in Israel, threatens both Christians and Muslims." In a reference to severe travel restrictions within the country, especially the 'security barrier' erected by the Israelis around the West Bank, he said: "We have a new generation of Christians that cannot visit the holy places of their faith, which are just a few kilometres from where they live."[167] The October 2010 Synod of Middle East Bishops in Rome reiterated concerns about the emigration of Christians and also underlined that people of all faiths were suffering from the effects of the continuing political problems in the region. While noting the "suffering and insecurity" of Israelis, a communiqué at the end of the conference also concluded: "We have taken account of the Israeli-Palestinian conflict on the whole region, especially on the Palestinians who are suffering the consequences of Israeli occupation: the lack of freedom of movement, the wall of separation and the military check-points, the political prisoners, the demolition of homes, the disturbance of socio-economic life and the thousands of refugees."[168]

75

The Israeli government has made it harder for foreign priests, religious, and seminarians to get visas. Visas are now valid only for one year instead of two. Franciscan priest Fr Pierbattista Pizzaballa, Custodian of the Holy Land, said: "There is a bit of confusion. We do not know whether it reflects ministerial policy or is due to certain officials dragging their feet. Perhaps it is an ambiguity that is intended." The visa problem has made it especially difficult for seminarians training for the Latin Patriarchate, whose jurisdiction covers Israel, the Palestinian Territories, Jordan and Cyprus. Students train at the Latin Patriarchate of Jerusalem seminary in Beit Jala, near Bethlehem. At present restrictions are growing, especially for Jordanians, who constitute two thirds of seminarians. Their visas are very often valid for only one entry. In the past, they had multiple-entry visas, enabling them to visit their families three or four times a year. In the case of Jordanians, these restrictions are seen as unwarranted as Jordan and Israel signed a peace treaty in 1994.

Christians also face difficulties in areas under the Palestinian National Authority, both in the West Bank but more especially in the Gaza Strip. Since Hamas took over Gaza in June 2007, Christians have come under pressure from Islamists to conform to Muslim practices. For example women have been forced to cover their heads in public and police have begun stopping Christians from selling alcohol. As Islamisation has increased, men have been banned from appearing bare-chested on Gaza's beaches. Clothes shops have been told to remove mannequins displaying lingerie.[169] Some Muslims regard Christians as a symbol of the West, and as such responsible for their problems. Christian homes, shops and churches have been attacked almost on a daily basis. In a massively overpopulated region of 1.5 million people – of whom half are children – there are no more than 5,000 Christians.[170]

The 22-day Israeli bombardment of Gaza in January 2009, aimed at stopping attacks from Hamas and other Islamist groups, left more than 1,100 people dead.[171] Aid to the Church in Need helped disaster-stricken people by providing emergency aid, which was distributed by Mgr Manuel Musallam, parish priest of Holy Family parish, in Gaza City. He described how people had suffered horrific injuries, saying "I have seen people with burnt faces – women and children." Many aid organisations noted children among the casualties. Although the Israelis only targeted military establishments, police stations and government buildings, many civilian targets were hit. Mgr Musallam described how a stray bomb landed in the playground of the school of the Rosary Sisters in Gaza City.[172] Israeli reports showed that 22,000 buildings were destroyed in damage estimated at US$1.9 billion (£1.16 billion, €1.36 billion).[173]

In the West Bank, Christians have been subject to pressure from Islamist groups whose appeal is growing among the population. Muslims have been buying up souvenir shops around the Basilica of the Nativity. "In the 1950s, there were very few mosques in the Bethlehem area," a local woman said. "Today, there are many more, built on purpose near Christian places of worship."[174]

February 2009: Israel's Channel 10 broadcast a programme that lampooned Jesus and the Virgin Mary. The Catholic bishops of the Holy Land condemned the programme, which they said directed its attack against the holiest figures of Christian belief in an attempt, as the director of the programme himself declared, to destroy Christianity. They said that Channel 10 had offended thousands of Christian Israeli citizens as well as millions of Christians all over the world. The bishops urged Channel 10 to "acknowledge its responsibility, and to apologise officially and publicly for this incident, and never to allow its repetition". They went on to call on the authorities to "take the appropriate measures against such unacceptable offence and its perpetrators".

April 2009: On Good Friday 2009, the Way of the Cross previously celebrated in the streets of Gaza had to be performed inside the Latin-rite Church of the Holy Family. Increased security concerns were given as the reason for the change.

May 2009: Professor Thiab Ayyoush, a leading expert on Christian-Muslim relations, was refused a permit to travel from the West Bank to Jerusalem, where the Pope was due to address an inter-faith conference as part of his Holy Land trip. Church authorities had sent the Muslim scholar a personal invitation to attend the event.[175]

May 2009: In Bethlehem, Pope Benedict XVI spoke about the Israeli 'security barrier', and urged Palestinians and Israelis to overcome "fear and mistrust". He said: "I have seen, adjoining the camp and overshadowing much of Bethlehem, the wall that intrudes into your territories, separating neighbours and dividing families... In a world where more and more borders are being opened up – to trade, to travel, to movement of peoples, to cultural exchanges – it is tragic to see walls still being erected. How we long to see the fruits of the much more difficult task of building peace! How earnestly we pray for an end to the hostilities that have caused this wall to be built! On both sides of the wall, great courage is needed if fear and mistrust is to be overcome, if the urge to retaliate for loss or injury is to be resisted."[176]

May 2009: Around 70 graves in Palestinian Christian cemeteries in the West Bank village of Jiffna were desecrated by vandals. Greek Orthodox Church official George Abdo said: "When we arrived this morning to attend Holy Mass, we were surprised by the desecration of the graves of the Christian dead in this cemetery. Out of the 200 graves, about 70 were destroyed and their crosses broken. This is the first time Christian property has been attacked by trouble-makers attempting to create a bad mood in society here." No group claimed responsibility for the attack.[177]

August 2009: In late August, schools in Gaza City imposed a new dress code on girls, requiring them to wear jilbab, traditional Islamic sleeved robes, and to cover their hair. Boys and girls were separated and put into different buildings. The rules were also enforced on the Christian minority in state schools. Thus far, however, private Christian schools have been made exempt.[178]

December 2009: Yossi Yomtov, a Christian of Jewish ethnic origin, sought police protection after having been attacked four times because of his faith. The Jerusalem resident said police had been slow to investigate the hate crimes against him. In two of the attacks a youth attacked him with pepper spray and stun gun shocks.[179]

December 2009: A report entitled *A Moment of Truth (Kairos Palestine)*, released by the World Council of Churches, and endorsed by the bishops and heads of churches in Jerusalem, stressed the need for freedom of religion for everyone. The report said: "Trying to make the state a religious state, Jewish or Islamic, suffocates the state, confines it within narrow limits, and transforms it into a state that practises discrimination and exclusion, preferring one citizen over another. We appeal to both religious Jews and Muslims: let the state be a state for all its citizens, with a vision constructed on respect for religion but also on equality, justice, liberty and respect for pluralism, and not on domination by a religion or a numerical majority."

April 2010: During Easter celebrations, Israeli authorities limited the number of permits for Christians from the West Bank and Gaza who wanted to travel to Jerusalem. Fr Raed Abousahlia, Catholic parish priest in Taybeh, in the West Bank, said he could only get 200 permits for the members of his congregation, one third of the allocation for previous years. In Ramallah, Greek Orthodox Bishop Atallah Hanna said that Israel's attitude showed a desire "to violate religious freedom... Jerusalem must remain an open city for all Christians." Yusef Daher of the World Council of Churches said Israelis were calling into question the tradition of religious freedom, which has held for the past 900 years.

March 2010: The Palestinian Authority reversed a decision to close down several private TV and radio stations, including Christian broadcaster Al-Mahed TV. It came a week after the Palestinian Authority closed the stations, claiming their owners had failed to pay fees to renew the licences for their stations. Al-Mahed TV's owner-manager, Samir Qumsia, condemned the decision, saying he had sent a letter to Palestinian Authority President Mahmoud Abbas and Prime Minister Salam Fayyad protesting against the closures.[180]

May 2010: Auxiliary Bishop William Shomali of the Latin Patriarchate of Jerusalem said the 14 million Christians living in the Middle East had a duty to foster peace and coexistence, despite difficulties and persecution. Bishop Shomali stressed the need for Christians of the Middle East to see their presence as a vocation, avoiding being shut in a "ghetto mentality", which might lead increasingly to social obscurity. In his lecture, entitled "The Middle Eastern Synod in its Geopolitical and Pastoral Context", the new auxiliary Bishop of Jerusalem analysed the situation of minorities in each country.[181]

October 2010: Arsonists set fire to a church in Jerusalem. The basement windows of the Alliance Church Ministry Centre were broken into and its lower floors set on fire. Volunteer workers from the US and Denmark sleeping at the church's overnight facilities were sent to a nearby hospital to be treated for smoke inhalation. The fire largely gutted the basement and destroyed recent renovations.[182]

Kazakhstan

Population	Religions	Christian Population
15.5 million	Muslim 50% Atheists 30% Christians 15% Other 5%	2.5 million

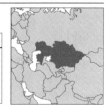

Despite Kazakhstan becoming the first Muslim majority country, and the first former Soviet state to assume the leadership of the Organisation of Security and Cooperation in Europe (OSCE), it continued to violate its public commitment to allow freedom of religion. Documented violations included censorship of religious literature, restrictions on religious freedom, raids, interrogations, threats and fines, restrictions on social and charitable activities by religious communities, heavy surveillance and attempts to confiscate property.

Many groups, including religious communities, experience difficulties obtaining registration and those that fail face grave problems which considerably limit their activities. Groups belonging to the Council of Baptist Churches refuse to register, considering this undue interference in religious affairs. The UN expert on minority affairs, Gay McDougall, who visited Kazakhstan in July 2009, said: "The existing law on registration of religious organisations and activities should be brought into compliance with the Constitution of the Republic [of Kazakhstan] and international legal standards… Repressive measures against religious groups and their members must stop immediately."[183]

Fears over the increasing influence of Islamic fundamentalism have caused the parliament to draft new legislation restricting religious freedom. Before signing it into law, President Nazarbayev submitted it to the Constitutional Court. In February 2009, Igor Rogov, President of the Constitutional Council, declared the law unconstitutional. He said the legislation violated the constitution's defence of the people's secular and religious rights. The law would have explicitly banned unregistered religious activities and obliged all religious organisations to re-register.

Towards the end of 2009, the government brought a proposal before parliament to modify the Administrative Code. But the two articles that affect religious groups were left substantially unaltered. Article 374.1 declares the state's determination to punish those involved in unregistered social and religious organisations, including managers and donors. Article 375 meanwhile punishes "violations of the law on religions" including missionary activity without state authorisation. A new crime of inciting "religious superiority" (new Article 405) is being included in the government's draft law.

February 2009: Baptist pastor Yuri Rudenko from Almaty Region was the third unregistered minister to be jailed for three days for refusing to pay fines for carrying out an unauthorised service. Baptist churches in Akmola region were been raided and their members questioned.[184]

June 2009: Baptist pastor Vasily Kliver was given a five-day jail sentence for refusing to pay fines for leading unregistered worship in Aktobe. Before he was arrested, the pastor's flat was searched and his refrigerator was confiscated in part payment for the fine.

June 2009: Protestant pastor Maksim Tashenov was fined the equivalent of US$80 (£50, €60) for participating in religious activity in a different region of Kazakhstan to that where his own church is registered. He was prosecuted after a police raid on the church.[185]

July 2009: Anti-terrorism officers filmed a religious service and questioned children belonging to the New Life Full Gospel Pentecostal Church in Aktau. One church member was sacked from her job in a school, interrogated and threatened when officers tried to recruit her as a spy. She was fined for "illegal missionary activity".[186]

July 2009: Following an initiative taken by President Nursultan Nazarbayev, the 3rd Congress of the Leaders of World Religions and Traditions was held in Astana. The congress was dedicated to reflecting on the role played by religions in fostering greater tolerance, respect and cooperation.

July 2009: There were reports of Catholic priests ministering in Kazakhstan facing difficulties gaining access to institutions, including prisons.[187]

August 2009: The Baptist congregation in Rudny, in the Kostanai region, had their entire service filmed by officers from the Criminal Police Department. Church members were subsequently interviewed individually.

A few days afterwards the film was broadcast with a negative commentary on the regional television channel. The church's pastor was then fined the equivalent of US$390 (£250, €290).

August 2009: Police raided a house in Uspen where local Christians were meeting with visiting members of the Pavlodar Grace Church. Police questioned one visitor and allegedly beat local woman Safura Mil until she signed a document stating she had been forced to submit to a religious ritual. Two of the visitors, Kayrat Zhgangozhin and Ramil Imankulov, were charged with "having forced people to hold religious services or take part in other religious activities." Police Inspector Nurserik Aytzhanov told Forum 18: "They were imposing their religion on the residents of the town by saying that 'Jesus Christ is the only God and you must believe in him'... Such preaching is prohibited by our law." He denied anyone was beaten by police.[188]

August 2009: Four Baptists in the Syrym district of the city of Jambeyt – Ivan Isayev, Sergei Krasnov, K. Batimov, and N. Maksina – who were visiting friends, were fined the equivalent of US$390 (£250, €290), about 50 times the minimum wage, for unregistered religious activity.

November 2009: Feruza Utegenova, a member of New Life Church in Aktau, who stood trial after giving a 12-year-old girl a Christian children's newspaper, lost her appeal against deportation. Deported back to her native Uzbekistan, she is now cut off from her four grown-up children.[189]

November 2009: Viktor Leven, who was born in Kazakhstan but who holds a German passport, was deported for leading worship of a Baptist congregation in Akmola. As a German citizen, he was accused of having performed missionary activities without the necessary state authorisation. Initially, in October 2009, Leven won his appeal, but later the regional court in Akmola reinstated the deportation order. Deportation separated him from his wife and their six children, the youngest being just three weeks old.[190]

December 2009: A Protestant pastor is facing criminal charges for "causing severe damage to health, due to negligence". He is said to have agreed to a church member's request to pray together for her health to improve.[191]

December 2009: Newspapers in Akmola ran an article by "anti-cult" activist Gulnara Orazbaeva, accusing Baptists of spreading the Bird Flu

(H1N1) virus. She accused David Leven – brother of Baptist pastor Viktor Leven – of causing the death of one of his children and preventing his pregnant wife from going to hospital when she was in labour.[192]

December 2009: In the eastern region of Beskaraga, the Spiritual Centre for the Rehabilitation of Drug Addicts and Alcoholics was closed by Beskaraga district court and its founder and director, Christian Sergei Mironov, was fined the equivalent of about US$1,550 (£1,000, €1,190). Activities were initially halted in January when the centre, registered since 2006 as a public association, was accused of carrying out unauthorised religious activities and of having converted people to Christianity.

February 2010: People exercising freedom of religion and belief would still be subject to punishment according to a revised version of a proposed administrative code. The amended document continues to prescribe fines for unregistered religious activities. It also leaves in place a ban on unauthorised religious "foreigners" conducting unapproved missionary activity, who would still face fines and deportation. A new offence of inciting "religious superiority" was also included in the draft.[193]

May 2010: There were reports of Catholic clergy facing problems with visa regulations, meaning that they were delayed as they were preparing to enter the country.[194]

June 2010: Religious groups expressed concern about a school Religious Studies textbook which, in the words of one local specialist, contains "aggressive, sometimes insulting and even offensive" language about some Kazakh religious communities. Among those who have expressed concern are Ahmadis, Protestants, Hare Krishna devotees, Jehovah's Witnesses and the state Religious Affairs Committee.[195]

Laos

Population	Religions	Christian Population
6.5 million	Buddhist 50% Local religions 45% Christians 3% Other 2%	200,000

Although the country's constitution guarantees religious freedom, a 2002 Prime-Ministerial Decree requires official approval for most religious activities, including evangelisation, printing, building places of worship, and contacts with foreign religious groups. Those accused of religious offences can be arrested and held without trial. Christian groups are particularly targeted, often because they are seen as connected to the West.

The government only recognises three Christian communities: The Lao Evangelical Church; the Catholic Church; and the Seventh-day Adventists. There are 150,000 Protestants in the country, mostly members of the Lao Evangelical Church. According to the findings of a November 2010 Aid to the Church in Need fact-finding trip to Laos, the Catholic Church has about 40,000 faithful, led by four bishops and 16 priests – including two well beyond the age of retirement. All churches have their affairs scrutinised by the state. The largest Catholic gathering in the country's history took place in April 2010 when thousands were present for an Episcopal ordination in Thankek – a hopeful sign for the future,

Non-registered Christian communities meanwhile continued to face problems. Arrests and detentions of members of un-authorised churches occurred during 2009-10 in Luang Namtha, Phongsali, and Savannakhet provinces. (Each of the country's 16 provinces (*khoueng*) is subdivided into districts (*muang*) and then subdivided into administrative regions or "villages" (*baan*).) Local officials reportedly pressured Protestants to renounce their faith or risk arrest or eviction from villages in the provinces of Bolikhamxai, Houaphan, Salavan, Luang Prabang, Attapeu, Oudomxai, and Luang Namtha.[196]

A number of Christians – both Catholic and Protestant – belong to ethnic groups such as the *Mon-Kher* and the *Hmong* and ethnic tensions are a factor in the difficulties they face. The *Hmong*, who live in the mountainous regions, continue to be targeted by the military, because of their historic opposition to Communism.

84

June-July 2009: Elders of Katin village in Ta-Oy district, Saravan province, told 53 Christians to renounce their faith or face "serious consequences". Following the warning, officials and residents confiscated and slaughtered pigs belonging to nine Christian families. Officials stated that the seizure of the livestock – worth six weeks' wages for a labourer – was a punishment for not abandoning Christianity.[197]

November 2009: 26 people died during army attacks against Christians, Buddhists and Animists in the Phou Bia Mountain area of Xieng Kjouang Province. Hundreds were believed to be injured and without any medical care. There were at least 118 women and children hiding in the jungle. Earlier, churches and temples in the area had been forcibly closed.[198]

January 2010: At Katin village in Ta-Oy district, about 100 people – including local officials and police – held Christians at gunpoint during a Sunday morning service. Officials confiscated all belongings from 11 houses belonging to Christians, destroying six of the dwellings. Worshippers were forced to walk nearly four miles (6 km) from the village and police were posted at the entrance to stop them returning. Church members, including children, had to sleep rough in the woods with little food or equipment. This followed a long-running campaign by the mostly pagan villagers to force the Christians to renounce their beliefs.[199]

April 2010: Catholics gathered for the episcopal ordination of Jean Marie Inthirath Prida, as Vicar Apostolic of Savannakhet in St Louis Cathedral, Thakhek, on the banks of the Mekong river. Mgr. Prida thanked "Mother Church" for never having forgotten Lao Catholics.[200]

April 2010: One of the Christians expelled from Katin village in January 2010 died after families suffered a shortage of food and clean water, which caused an outbreak of diarrhoea, dehydration, eye and skin infections, fainting and general weakness.[201]

November 2010: Officials in Katin village ordered six more Christian families to renounce their faith or face expulsion.[202]

January 2011: Police arrested 11 Christians at gunpoint in the Hinboun district of Khammouan Province, on Tuesday 4th. Six were released from the provincial prison the following day, including two children aged 4 and 8, but three house church leaders remain in prison for "holding a secret meeting". The charge is a political offense punishable by law.[203]

Lebanon

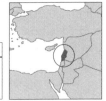

Population	Religions	Christian Population
4.3 million	Muslim 53% Christian 43% Other 4%	1.9 million

Christians are emigrating as Lebanon becomes increasingly Islamicised. In 2009 Fr Samir Khalil SJ, founder of the Centre for Arab Christian Research and Documentation, reported that Christians had fallen to well below 50 percent of the population, adding that the situation was "worrying". Fr Khalil said Christians were emigrating to countries with larger Christian populations such as America and Australia, as well as countries in Europe.[204] The outlook for the Church is uncertain in a country with a uniquely strong and rich Christian culture. Violence is also a problem.

Shortly before Maronite Patriarch, Cardinal Nasrallah Sfeir's visit to the Beqaa Valley to consecrate a new church in June 2010, a bomb exploded killing one person and injuring two others. The device had been concealed in a storage room at a shop selling car parts. According to some sources, the prelate was the intended victim.

While religion continues to be a sensitive issue, the state has taken steps to ease tensions. In 2009 Interior Minister Ziad Baroud announced that citizens would no longer have religion included in their Vital Statistics files. This information was removed from identity papers after the Civil War as many Lebanese were abducted or killed because their identity papers displayed their religion.

Despite religious difficulties, article 9 of the Constitution establishes the State's respect for all religions and guarantees them autonomy for issues such as marriage and the family. Lebanon remains a leader in the Middle East with regard to respect for religious freedom. Faith groups are able to organise their own schools, associations and courts.

Key political appointments are allocated according to religious criteria: the president of the republic must be a Maronite Catholic; the president of the Council of Ministers a Sunni Muslim; and the parliamentary Speaker a Shiite Muslim. Religious communities are also represented in parliament according to fixed quotas. However there are moves towards secularisation. On 25th April 2010, the first pro-secularism rally was held in Beirut with about 5,000 people taking part. Many Christians fear secularisation would give Muslims, who are conscious of their majority status, an opportunity to dominate the main institutions of the state and of the administration.

At the start of 2011 there were up to 50,000 Iraqi refugees in Lebanon, many of them Christians, but they have been refused temporary legal status. Lebanon did not sign up to the 1951 International Convention on Refugees and does not accept foreign refugees on its territory, other than those to whom the UN has granted a temporary permit while waiting to resettle them in another country. According to the UN High Commissioner for Refugees: "Most of the registered Iraqi refugees in Lebanon do not wish to return home but may be compelled to do so if the authorities apply stricter policies towards them. At the same time, the unstable situation in some parts of Iraq may increase the number of asylum-seekers arriving from the country."[205]

November 2009: The announcement of plans for a Spiritual Centre in Kobayat, northern Lebanon, was hailed as a key initiative to stem the decline of Christianity. Central to the ACN-supported project is the renovation of former monastery and school buildings and the development of a conference centre, seminar rooms, two refectories, dormitories, living quarters as well as a chapel.[206]

February 2010: During a visit to Rome, Archbishop Georges Bacouni of Tyre said: "Christians are facing major challenges and various problems due to the many changes that affect not only Lebanon, but the entire Middle East. Particularly from the point of view of Catholics, we are faced with a decline in the number of believers, [this is a] time of crisis that creates negative consequences on the process of integration for Christians in a land… in which their presence is diminishing over time. What is even more surprising, compared to the last century, is the reduction of the Christian presence within the political institutions in social sectors, in education, as well as within the ranks of the military." He said the Christian minority are finding it increasingly difficult to integrate, as they find themselves "situated in a hotbed of unrest, something that produces a climate of widespread fear among the local population".[207]

February 2010: Pope Benedict XVI told Lebanese Prime Minister Saad Hariri that Lebanon was a model of coexistence and, echoing the words of Pope John Paul II, said it was a "message" for the entire Middle East. The statement was made during a visit by Prime Minister Hariri to the Vatican.[208]

March 2010: Maronite Patriarch, Nasrallah Sfeir met the Pope and participated in the preparatory work of the Synod of the Churches of the Middle East. He spoke of the need for coordination "among all the living forces of Lebanon" including the army and Hezbollah, saying "these forces must obey the rules. We must respect the rules that the government and public opinion consider mandatory."[209]

March 2010: For the first time Lebanese Christians and Muslims celebrated the Christian feast of the Annunciation as a national bank holiday. The decision to hold the holiday was confirmed during the meeting between Pope Benedict XVI and Prime Minister Hariri at the Vatican. The Council of Maronite Bishops said the celebration "is a unique event which deserves praise" for "it shows the face of Lebanon [as] 'the message'" and also "the place and honour occupied by the Virgin Mary in Christianity and Islam."[210]

June 2010: One person was killed and two others were injured in a night-time bomb blast in the predominantly Christian town of Zahle. The blast occurred several hours before a visit by Maronite Patriarch Nasrallah Sfeir to the town.[211]

June 2010: Islamist leaflets threatening Christians were widely distributed in the coastal town of Sidon. The leaflets said Christians should "spare their lives by evacuating the area within one week" or "bear the consequences". To prevent trouble soldiers were dispatched as the deadline for Christians to leave approached. Two suspects were arrested. [212]

July 2010: Ahmad Hariri, secretary general of Sunni political party the Future Movement, which is part of the ruling coalition, urged Muslims in Lebanon to "nurture the Christian presence" in the region, saying it was an "Arab and Islamic responsibility as much as it is a Christian one". *The Jerusalem Post* reported that Hariri is extremely concerned by the repercussions of Christian emigration from the region.[213]

Maldives

Population	Religions	Christian Population
315,000	Muslim 99% Other 1%	Unknown[214]

This nation, made up of more than 1,000 islands, has a system of institutionalised intolerance towards non-Muslims which has deepened in recent years. In late 2010, religious freedom observers listed Maldives as among the five countries where anti-Christian persecution was worst.[215] At about the same time, the US State Department declared that in the archipelago "freedom of religion is restricted significantly".[216] The 2008 constitution bans all religious practices other than Islam. Non-Muslim foreigners are only allowed to pray in private and are strictly forbidden from encouraging citizens away from Islam. This also applies to the 675,000 tourists (mainly European and Japanese) who visit the Maldives every year. The constitution prevents non-Muslims from voting and holding public positions. It also states that a "non-Muslim may not become a citizen of the Maldives". Some commentators hoped that President Mohamed Nasheed, who was elected in 2008, would reverse some of the restrictions on religious freedom in the country, but this has not yet happened.[217] Operating under the guidelines of the Religious Unity Act, in May 2010, the Ministry of Islamic Affairs introduced new regulations providing the legal framework for religious practice. All citizens must be Muslims and government initiatives must conform to Islamic *Shari'a* law.

Over the last three decades a more puritanical form of Islam has been brought in by students returning to the Maldives after studying in Islamic universities in Egypt, Saudi Arabia and Pakistan.[218] Reports show that women increasingly veil their faces and men grow beards, neither of which are traditional practices in the historically Islamic country. Several public demonstrations calling for the introduction of flogging have taken place in the capital, Male.[219]

Some 80,000 migrant workers – mostly Buddhists, Christians, Hindus and Muslims, from South Asia – make up about a quarter of the country's population, but in practice they are prevented from following their religion. Although migrant workers are officially allowed to practise their faith privately in their living quarters, most migrants are domestic helpers living with their employers, and therefore have no privacy in which to practise their faith. Customs officers search luggage for "un-Islamic" books, CDs, images, and other religious items. People have even been asked to remove small crosses worn as jewellery.[220]

November 2009: President Mohammed Nasheed said the spread of militant Islam in the country is drawing young people into extremist groups. During his visit to India he claimed "hundreds of Maldivians" have been recruited by the Taliban and are fighting in Pakistan. He made his remarks in an interview on the CNN-IBN news channel.[221]

November 2009: The Maldives parliament, the Majlis, unanimously approved the primary stages of a bill banning all non-Muslim places of worship, including proposed penalties of large fines and lengthy imprisonment.[222]

February 2010: Local press reported that the Ministry of Education asked an Indian teacher to leave the country for allegedly preaching Christianity to her students. It came two months after an American family was deported after being suspected of carrying out missionary work. According to police, although no formal charges were filed, the practice was to send the people back to their country of origin while the case was being investigated.

April 2010: The Ministry of Islamic Affairs proposed the introduction of comparative religion at university level. But the religiously conservative Adhaalath Party opposed the proposal, stating that comparative religion should not be taught until the public's understanding of the basic principles of Islam is strengthened.[223]

October 2010: Open Doors, a Protestant human rights organisation, released a report listing Maldives as the fifth-worst country for persecution of Christians. Since Open Doors' 2001 report the Maldives climbed from nine to five in its list of countries where Christians are most badly oppressed.[224]

Nigeria

Population	Religions	Christian Population
158 million	Muslim 40% Christian 40% Local religions 20%	63 million

Despite the Nigerian constitution guaranteeing religious freedom and forbidding the adoption of a state religion, the country has been a member of the Conference of Islamic States since 1986, and *Shari'a* law is applied in 12 of Nigeria's 36 states (Bauchi, Borno, Gombe, Jigawa, Kaduna, Kano, Katsina, Kebbi, Niger, Sokoto, Yobe and Zamfara). Criminal offences can be punished with flogging, amputation of limbs, and even the death sentence. Archbishop Ignatius Kaigama of Jos said: "Since the introduction of the *Shari'a* in its present form, there has been great tension, there has been an uneasy relationship and this has erupted into violence sometimes."[225]

In principle, *Shari'a* law does not apply to non-Muslims, but Christians in the 12 *Shari'a* states have complained of widespread discrimination. The problems reported include false charges of blasphemy against Islam; Christian students and teachers being forced to leave schools; refusal for permits to build churches and the demolition of supposedly unlawfully built places of worship – over 300 churches have been destroyed in the last four years;[226] the abduction and forced conversion of teenagers, especially girls who are then married to Muslims; discrimination against Christians in public sector employment and in access to public services; the imposition of Islamic dress code on Christian female students; and priority given to Muslims in public schools and universities. At least four states (Zamfara, Niger, Kaduna and Kano) have set up a religious police (*Hisbah*) to enforce Islamic standards in public life.

The area around Jos has continued to be unstable. Massacres in Jos and its surrounding villages (on 21st February and 7th March 2010 respectively) led to controversy over who carried them out and whether they were religiously motivated. According to Archbishop Kaigama, poverty and inter-tribal tensions were the key factors behind February's clashes. [227] However, the later attack, in which Christian women and children were killed, was carried out by Fulani Muslim herdsmen from neighbouring Bauchi State, wanting revenge for the earlier violence.

November 2008: Following allegations of fraud in local elections, members of the largely Muslim Hausa ethnic group launched violent protests against Christians, who generally backed the winning People's Democratic Party. At least 400 people died. 40 churches and several mosques were destroyed.

February 2009: In Bauchi State, violence broke out between Christians and Muslims after a truck broke down in a road between a Pentecostal church and a mosque, blocking the path of Muslims going to Friday prayers. 11 people died and 1,500 were made homeless. In total, 14 churches, eight presbyteries, two mosques and about 150 homes and shops were damaged or destroyed. The exact cause of the violence remains unknown.

April 2009: Muslim groups in Niger State attacked an Easter procession, injuring 20 Christians and setting fire to three churches in Gwada city.

July 2009: Security forces clashed with extremist Islamist group Boko Haram. It followed reports that the group was stockpiling armaments in a bid to overthrow government institutions in northern Nigeria, impose *Shari'a* law, and outlaw "western education". The ensuing violence spread to five states – Borno, Bauchi, Gombe, Kano and Yobe. 700 people died.

September 2009: Bishop Timothy Joseph Carroll, the Apostolic Vicar to Kontagora in Niger State, denounced the destruction by Islamist militants of churches under construction.

December 2009: The crackdown by security forces against the Kala-Kato Islamist group in the city of Bauchi left 70 people dead. The Kala-Kato reject various aspects of modern life, including "western education", medicine, radio, television and all books, except for the *Qur'an*.

January 2010: Up to 500 people died during three days of inter-religious violence in Jos. Most of those killed were Muslims. During the unrest, churches and mosques were attacked, and some 5,000 were made homeless.

January 2010: Three Pentecostal Churches (the Redeemed Christian Church of God, the Christian Faith Bible Church and the Living Faith Foundation Chapel) were attacked by groups of young Muslims in Tudun Wada and Gusau, Zamfara State. No one was arrested.

February 2010: A Muslim mob attacked and set fire to eight buildings belonging to the Deeper Life Bible Church, the Apostolic Church, the

ECWA Church, the Redeemed Christian Church, the Word of Faith movement, the Assemblies of God, the Anglican Church and the Catholic Church. It followed an incident in which police in Kazaure (Jigawa State) killed a man driving a tractor.

March 2010: Fulani Muslims from Bauchi attacked three villages (Zot Foron, Dogo Nahawa and Rastat) inhabited by members of the Berom ethnic group (mainly Christians), some 9.5 miles (15 km) south of the city of Jos. More than 250 people were killed, including women and children, and 75 homes were set on fire.[228]

March 2010: Muslim extremists dressed as soldiers attacked two Christian villages in Plateau State, torching 20 houses and killing 13 people, mostly women (including one who was pregnant) and children. The victims had their tongues cut out.

April 2010: Two Christian journalists were stabbed to death north of Jos by a group of young Muslims, who talked about their crime on their victims' mobile phones. That same day four other Christians were killed by a gang of young Muslims. It came after the body of a Muslim teenager was found buried in the Christian village of Nasarawa Gwom.[229]

May 2010: More than 100 Muslim youths besieged church property in Kano state in northern Nigeria, destroying two church buildings and a minister's house belonging to the Evangelical Church Winning All (ECWA) at Kwasam, in the Kiru Local Government Area.[230]

July 2010: At least seven people, including a mother of six, were killed by Islamist militants in Kaduna. Armed men in military uniform killed seven Christians in Kizachi Dawai Chawai after surrounding the village at about 8.30pm on 3rd July and shooting indiscriminately. The following day, residents of Ganawuri village, near Jos in neighbouring Plateau state, were attacked by men wielding guns and machetes. Reports suggest the attackers may have been Fulani militants from Kaduna.[231]

December 2010: Nearly 40 people were killed and 74 were injured during attacks on Christmas Eve. In Jos city several bombs exploded, targeting Christmas shoppers. A bomb set to explode during Midnight Mass was defused by police. That same day, two churches in the northern city of Maiduguri were attacked, killing at least six people including a Baptist pastor and two choristers preparing for a carol service.[232]

North Korea

Population	Religions	Christian Pop.
24 million	Agnostic/Atheist: 70% New religions 13% Animist 13% Christian 2%, Others 2%	500,000

North Korea is described by human rights and Christian organisations as probably the most difficult place in the world to be a Christian.[233] That there should be any uncertainty about this is not so much because of doubts about the severity of persecution but rather a lack of evidence concerning a country largely sealed off from the world.

Although North Korea's constitution provides for "freedom of religious belief", in practice religious freedom does not exist. Kim Jong-il's regime tightly controls religious practice. Since the communist regime began in 1953, 300,000 Christians have disappeared. Nothing is known about the priests and nuns in North Korea at that time – they are assumed to be dead. In 2009 investigations by Human Rights Watch and the UN found that people caught praying – especially if it involved foreign organisations – were likely to be executed. In November 2009 two former prisoners – Guang-il Jung, 46, and Lee Ok Suk, 53 – told politicians in London and Brussels about conditions experienced by 200,000 people in North Korea's notorious camps. Prisoners were being subjected to torture, murder, rape, medical experimentation, forced labour and forced abortion. Religious detainees receive harsher treatment. In late 2010 US human rights monitors stated: "Defector reports indicated the government increased its investigation, repression and persecution of unauthorised religious groups."[234]

As with other religious groups, Christians are required to join party-controlled organisations. One Catholic and two Protestant churches exist in the capital, Pyongyang, but nothing is known about churches elsewhere. Catholics remain the only religious community without a minister. The Pope has declared the three North Korean dioceses – Pyongyang, Hamhung and Chunchon – to be vacant sees, under the administration of South Korean diocesan bishops appointed by Rome. In 2010 the Vatican still listed Francis Hong Yong-ho as Bishop of Pyongyang, but notes he is missing.[235] He has not been seen since 10th March 1962, and would be well over 100. However, the Vatican insists that it "cannot be excluded that he may still be a prisoner in some re-education camp".[236]

The government's clampdown on Christians looked set to increase at the end of 2010 as tension increased with South Korea. Both countries seemed on a collision course especially after North Korea shelled an island in the South, killing four people.[237]

June 2009: 33-year-old Christian Ri Hyon-ok was executed "for putting Bibles into circulation". Possessing a Bible is a crime that can carry the death penalty. She was also accused of spying for South Korea and the USA, and helping to organise dissidents. Her parents, husband, and children were sent to a prison camp.[238]

August 2009: Li Mingshun and Zhang Yonghu, both thought to be Chinese, were tried for aiding North Korean refugees fleeing to South Korea through China. They were among several Christians providing food, shelter, and transportation for the 61 refugees crossing into Mongolia in April 2009. After the trial, believed to have taken place in China, Ms Li and Mr Zhang received jail sentences for 10 years and seven years respectively.[239]

February 2010: Robert Park, a Korean-American missionary, was arrested and detained for 43 days. Originally from Tucson, Arizona, he crossed illegally into North Korea from China on Christmas Day 2009.[240]

May 2010: Lord Alton of Liverpool spoke about North Korea in the House of Lords. He said: "North Korea has experienced enforced disappearances, executions, arbitrary detentions, a lack of religious freedom, a lack of freedom of movement both domestically and internationally, a lack of labour rights, the non-implementation of legal codes, a lack of judicial oversight of detention facilities, the severe mistreatment of repatriated persons, violence against women in detention facilities, a lack of freedom for enterprise especially for farmers and food merchants, the lack of a fair trial, a lack of press freedom and a lack of the right to food for persons in prisons and labour camps."

August 2010: Reports stated that 23 Christians belonging to an underground church in Kuowoi-dong, Pyongsong City, South Pyongan Province were arrested. Three were executed and the rest sent to Yoduk prison camp.[241]

Pakistan

Population	Religions	Christian Population
175 million	Muslim 95% Christian 1.5% Hindu 1.5 Others 2%	2.5 million

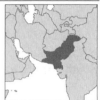

Six people – including two children – were burned alive in anti-Christian attacks on 1st August 2009. That same day, an elderly man – the children's grandfather – was shot dead. The killings happened as thousands of people rampaged through the Christian quarter of Gojra in the Punjab Province. It had been reported that Christians had cut up pages of the *Qur'an* to make wedding confetti. The mob, carrying sticks, clubs and firearms, attacked property including more than 150 homes and two churches.

This attack – *described in detail on pp103-04* – is one of many inextricably linked to the country's blasphemy laws (paragraphs B and C of Section 295 of Pakistan's Penal Code). Offences against the *Qur'an* receive a sentence of life imprisonment and insults against the Prophet Mohammed can be punished by death. According to the Catholic Church's National Commission for Justice and Peace (NCJP), between 1986 and 2010 at least 993 people were charged with either desecrating the *Qur'an* or slandering Mohammed. Most of the charges have been brought against Muslims: 479 of the accused were Muslims (many from the *Shia* group) and 340 were Ahmadis, an Islamic religious movement regarded by many orthodox Muslims as heretical. 120 of those accused were Christians

Reports show that the blasphemy laws are often invoked by people with a personal vendetta against a particular group or individual. Since 2001 at least 50 Christians have been killed by those using the blasphemy laws as a pretext. Accusations against alleged blasphemers are often false or motivated by petty interests, encouraging mobs to mete out rough justice without reference to the law.

The constitution states that the Islamic Republic of Pakistan is officially a secular country and a number of recent national laws have reiterated equality of citizens in the eyes of the law "without distinction based on race or creed". The People's Party, led by Asif Ali Zardari, Benazir Bhutto's widower and the country's current president, has often called for "religious tolerance" and "respect". However, the blasphemy laws and the (revised) *hudud* ordinance continue to inflict pain and hardship on religious minorities. Christian women have continued to suffer sexual violation at the hands of extremists, who assume that a combination of the law and societal values will protect them.

Issues of religious tolerance in Pakistan have changed beyond all recognition since partition, when the country was formed out of British India. In August 1947 the country's founding father, Mohammed Ali Jinnah, famously declared: "You may belong to any religion, caste or creed. That has nothing to do with the State." The situation could not have been more different by 2010. When early that year Aid to the Church in Need staff visited Pakistan on a fact-finding and project-assessment trip, Archbishop Lawrence Saldanhana, President of the country's Catholic Bishops' Conference, told them: "We are experiencing a Talibanisation of Islam. It is not so much that they are becoming more religious, rather that they are becoming more intolerant of others."

The floods of summer 2010 left a trail of misery on an unprecedented scale – 2,000 dead, one million homes destroyed and 21 million made homeless. But in a sign of how deep-seated the climate of oppression had become, the UN reported that the flood waters had been intentionally diverted into regions highly populated by minority groups, including Christians. Concerns about increasing intolerance were to reach a peak by the end of 2010 when, on a questionable pretext, a Christian, Asia Bibi, was found guilty of blasphemy. This case, the first of its kind to result in the death sentence, set alarm bells ringing about the country's direction in terms of politics and the law, as well as religion.

December 2008: A plot to detonate a bomb in Lahore's Sacred Heart Cathedral during Christmas Day Mass failed after a car containing explosives, apparently intended for the cathedral, accidently exploded three miles (5km) outside the city. Earlier, cathedral parish priest Fr Andrew Nisari received an anonymous letter demanding Catholics convert to Islam or "face the consequences".[242]

December 2008: 14-year-old Christian schoolgirl Shaj Taj was bundled into the back of a car by three men while she was on her way to school.

They took her to a hotel where she was raped before being forced at gunpoint to convert to Islam and agree to marry her rapist.[243]

April 2009: Nine-year-old Christian girl Nisha Javid's body was found in a canal not far from the family home in Essangri village, outside of Jaranawala, Faisalabad. A post-mortem revealed Nisha had been raped, and died after repeated blows to the head.[244]

May 2009: The Taliban attacked a Christian colony in Karachi. Pastor Salim Sadiq of Holy Spirit Church said: "They barged into our homes shouting 'death to infidels' and beat us, hurling murderous threats if we don't convert to Islam."[245]

July 2009: Imran Masih was charged with burning pages from the *Qur'an* in Hajwery, Punjab province. Bishop Joseph Coutts of Faislabad organised an inter-religious meeting to restore calm after a 1,000-strong mob burnt tyres outside Faisalabad district jail, where the 26-year-old Christian was being held, and called for his death. In March 2010 Imran Masih was sentenced to life imprisonment. [246]

July 2009: Following accusations that children had cut up the *Qur'an*, a large mob descended on Korian, demanding that their father, Taalib Masih, be hanged for blasphemy. The gang set fire to more than 70 homes and two small churches.[247]

August 2009: Seven people – including two children – were burned alive in anti-Christian attacks on 1st August, when nearly 3,000 people rampaged through the Christian quarter of Gojra in the Punjab Province. (*See p.103-04 for full story*).[248]

September 2009: A 19-year-old Christian was murdered while being detained at a jail in Sialkot district, Punjab province. When the body was released for burial, it was covered in marks on his torso and arms, apparently showing he had been severely beaten in custody.[249]

October 2009: Speaking at Aid to the Church in Need UK's Westminster Event, Bishop Joseph Coutts of Faisalabad said: "We [Christians] always experienced some form of discrimination but what we are seeing now is far more serious. We are living in a state of constant tension. But we will continue to give witness to Christ despite the difficulties that come from extremists. Even our suffering is a witness to Christ." The bishop, who a few days later presided at the opening of ACN's Scottish office, went on to say: "We feel very encouraged when we know that we are not alone, when we see that there is somebody behind us, helping us, praying for us."

November 2009: St Denys Girls' School in Murree, run by the Church of Pakistan, was burned to the ground. The attack was suspected to be the work of fundamentalists.[250]

December 2009: Some 50 Muslim extremists armed with clubs and axes attacked the premises of the Catholic Church in Chak, Sargodha, during a showing of the "Jesus Film". Seven people were injured. Officers at Saddr police station refused to register a case against the assailants.[251]

January 2010: Rawalpindi police arrested Hector Aleem, 51, on charges of sending a text message insulting the prophet Mohammed. Allegedly, police assaulted him as well as his wife and two daughters. They removed 50,000 rupees worth of valuables and broke images of Jesus.[252]

January 2010: 12-year-old Christian girl Shazia Bashir died after being taken to Jinnah Hospital in Lahore, displaying signs of violence and torture. The girl's parents had been forbidden to see her by her employer, Chaudhry Naeem, for several days before her death. Thousands attended the funeral in Lahore. The following day her former employer Chaudhry Naeem appeared in court.[253]

March 2010: Six people were killed in an attack on the office of Christian charity World Vision in the Mansehra district. The charity said it would suspend all operations in the country.[254]

March 2010: Six men in Khanewal district, southern Punjab Province, axed 36-year-old Rasheed Masih to death for refusing to convert to Islam. Allegedly they grew resentful of his potato business, and killed him after inviting him to their farmhouse. His body was left on the roadside near Kothi Nand Singh village early the following day.[255]

April 2010: Marwat Masih, a Christian barber in Sargodha, Punjab Province, sustained broken bones and other injuries after eight Muslims beat him for shaving off the beard of 19-year-old Mulim Qandeel Cheema. Mr Cheema had requested his beard be shaved, and Mr Masih only complied after learning he would be leaving immediately. Neighbouring shopkeeper Muhammad Maqsood said: "[Mr Cheema] deserves such

99

punishment, as he did something that is forbidden according to the teaching of the *Qur'an* and the sunna."[256]

April 2010: On Easter Sunday, 10 Christian men were beaten in Sargodha, Punjab province, and despite being injured, were booked by police. The Christians had protested about the way some local Muslims had verbally abused Christian women going to the Easter Sunday Service at the Catholic Church in Virk Colony.[257]

May 2010: At least five Christian boys were forced to leave their homes in the Green Town area of Lahore after they were accused of blasphemy. They were asked by local Muslims to leave the area or face legal action for allegedly "desecrating" a banner inscribed with Qur'anic verses. Apparently the boys picked the banner up after it fell down due to strong winds.[258]

May 2010: John Gill, a Christian moulding machine operator at Shah Plastic Manufacturers in the Youhanabad area of Lahore, was forced to sell a kidney by his Muslim employer, Ghulam Mustafa, to pay a debt he owed him. Mr Gill was being charged 400 percent interest. Mr Mustafa came to Mr Gill's home with "about five armed men" and transported him to Ganga Ram hospital, where they forced him to sell the kidney. The value of the kidney was estimated at around 200,000 rupees, leaving Mr Gill with an outstanding debt of about 250,000 rupees.[259]

May 2010: Around 20 Islamic extremists gathered at the home of Atiq Joseph and Qaiser William and their wives, who had recently moved into a house in Gulshan-e-Iqbal town, Karachi. The couples had gathered a large pile of rubbish, including bits of old newspapers, left by the previous occupiers. Local resident Bashir Pervezi said: "I was standing in front of the new Christian tenants' house while 20 bearded, armed Muslim men arrived and started searching for something in the garbage." He said that after about 35 minutes they started shouting at the women, threatening to kill family members for desecrating the *Qur'an* by putting it in the rubbish. Mrs Joseph and Mrs William subsequently went through every scrap of paper but found nothing. On May 28th, a judge directed police to file charges against the couples, who had gone into hiding.[260]

June 2010: Up to 250 Christians were ordered to leave their homes in Katcha Khoh, in the Khanewal district of the Punjab province, after objecting to sexual assaults on girls and women. The order for them to leave was given by Muslim village head Abdul Sattar Khan after four Christian men complained about certain Muslim employers routinely using their positions to sexually assault Christian women and girls. The Christians said they did not file a complaint with police as they feared this would lead to false allegations of "blasphemy" being levelled at them.[261]

June 2010: Psychology professor Samuel John, who taught at the university in Khyber-Pakhtunkhwa Province for 12 years, was attacked at 8.30am on by 20-25 students housed on the university campus. They also turned on the professor's wife as she shouted for help. Both were rushed to hospital, where the professor was placed on the critical list. He had previously complained to university authorities that five students had threatened him if he did not convert to Islam. The university took no action. Prof John subsequently had stones thrown at his home and received threatening phone calls. The professor had recently been honoured with an award for his students' results, and it is thought that Muslims were upset by a Christian receiving such an accolade.[262]

July 2010: Christian nurse Magdaline Ashraf, 22, was gang raped by Dr Jabbar Memon, a Muslim doctor whom she had previously reported for harassing her, and two other men, at the Jinnah Postgraduate Medical Centre in Karachi. After raping the nurse they threw her out of the window. She was found unconscious on the lawn and taken to the on-site Intensive Care Unit. She recovered consciousness a few days later but remained in a critical condition.[263]

July 2010: Pastor Rashid Emmanuel, 32, and his brother Sajid, 24, were shot dead outside court where they were due to be tried for writing a pamphlet critical of the Prophet Mohammed. Khurram Shehzad alleged that one of his employees was handed a pamphlet at Faisalabad's general bus stand, containing disrespectful remarks about Mohammed, and giving contact details for the brothers. A police officer escorting the brothers was critically injured when the gunmen opened fire. At least 10 people were reportedly injured when rioting broke out in a Christian neighbourhood shortly afterwards.[264]

July 2010: At Lahorianwali, Narang Mandi, a small village near Sheikhupura, Punjab Province, a church building and Christian homes came under threat of demolition when Islamists, accompanied by local police, attempted to demolish them with a bulldozer. According to a Christian, Zulfiqar Gill: "They said that if we ever tried to rebuild the walls or renovate the frail Apostolic Church building, they would create a scene here like Gojra."[265]

October 2010: Vehari Emmanuel Masih, an 80-year-old Christian in southern Punjab Province, and his 75-year-old wife, were beaten, breaking his arms and legs and her skull, because he refused to have sex with a prostitute. Muslim land owners brothers Muhammad Malik Jutt and Muhammad Khaliq Jutt, accompanied by two other men, brought a prostitute to Mr Masih's house and ordered him to have sex with the woman. They attacked the Masihs when he refused. The couple were initially rushed to Tehsil Headquarters Hospital Burewala in a critical condition, but doctors allegedly turned them away at the behest of the Jutt brothers. Police only registered a case against the Jutt brothers after the intervention of Bekat and Albert Patras, directors of human rights group Social Environment Protection.[266]

November 2010: Asia Bibi, a Christian and mother of five was given the death sentence after being found guilty of blaspheming against the Prophet Mohammed. Asia, a farm labourer, was alleged to have made disparaging remarks about the prophet after fellow workers asked her to justify her faith. At the instigation of Auxiliary Bishop Sebastian Shaw of Lahore, Pope Benedict XVI publicly appealed for her life to be saved. Speaking later in an interview with Aid to the Church in Need, Bishop Shaw cast doubt on the credibility of the case against Asia by stating that in the initial phases she had no defence lawyer. President Asif Ali Zardari was urged to use his prerogative and pardon Asia but legal experts said this would only be possible after a High Court appeal. Meantime, Maulana Yousef Quresh, an imam from Peshawar, offered a reward of 500,000 rupees (US$5,853) for Asia to be killed.[267]

January 2011: Salman Taseer, Governor of the Punjab, was shot dead, apparently by one of his own bodyguards. The security official was said to have beem angered by Mr Taseer's stated criticism of the Blasphemy Laws. Mr Taseer had recently called on Pesident Zardari to pardon Asia Bibi, a Christian woman on death row after being ground guilty under the blasphemy laws. Mr Taseer had visited Asia Bibi in custody. The killing coincided with demonstrations in support of the blasphemy laws.[268]

Profile: Almas Hameed from Gojra, Pakistan

Almas Hameed lost seven members of his family – including his wife, two of his children, his father and a brother – as anti-Christian violence swept the Pakistan city of Gojra. He was forced into hiding after receiving death threats for implicating certain politicians in the attacks. During a March 2010 project-assessment and fact-finding trip to Pakistan, ACN met Almas in a safe house and heard his story.

For Almas, 1st August 2009 is a day that will live in infamy. It began with tension running high in the Punjab city of Gojra, 30 miles (50 km) from Faisalabad. Only two days earlier, Christians in the nearby village of Korian had come under fire from extremists outraged at an allegation of blasphemy against Islam. Up to 70 homes had been attacked, but there was no loss of life. 48 hours later in Gojra, Muslims began to gather for Friday prayers in the usual way. The mood suddenly changed. A procession got underway amid anger following reports that a Christian man and his son had desecrated pages with verses of the *Qur'an* to make confetti for a wedding. Christians were declared national enemies and were denounced as 'kafirs' (unbelievers) and 'dogs'.

News of the disturbance soon reached the family of Almas Hameed, well known to inhabitants of Gojra. The family's success in the building trade meant they had a smarter home than most of their Christian neighbours. As the huge procession made its way towards Gojra's Christian quarter, fear began to turn to panic. The police were trying to control the crowds but were struggling in the intense heat of the sun. Seeing their plight, Almas' father, Hameed Masih, stepped forward to offer the police a drink. Almas recalled what happened next: "While my father was giving the police a drink, somebody shot him. It happened just outside our house. As he lay dying, everyone – especially the family – started crying."

The family's first thought was to flee to the nearest church. But they soon learned the mob had got there first. He said: "People went into the church, grabbed the cross and began smacking it with their shoes. Then they started burning Bibles and carrying out other acts of desecration."

103

Suddenly shooting broke out and Christian homes were set on fire. Desperate to protect their own house, Almas and his family turned back and went home. But it was too late; their house was looted and there was nothing they could do to stop it. Almas remembers: "We thought: it's better not to interfere – that way at least we're safe. We stayed in the house and hoped they would go away." Family members locked themselves in various rooms of the house to protect themselves. But this proved fatal. Attackers sprayed flammable chemicals on the house and set it ablaze. Almas was able to rescue two of his children – Anosh, 13 and eight-year-old Kasia. Together, they clambered onto the roof. It saved their lives. Below them, other family members died in the blaze. In addition to Almas' father, Hameed, the dead included: Almas' wife, Asifa, 30, their children, Umaya, 11, and three-year-old Musa and Almas' brother, Akhlas. Also dead were Almas' sister-in-law, Asia Moshin, 25, and her mother, Parveen Victor.

In total 50 houses were burned and more than 100 other homes were looted by protestors. The government moved quickly to repair and rebuild Christian homes damaged in the violence. It helped to temper widespread anger among Christians at alleged police inaction during the incidents. In the days that followed, 200 people were arrested amid reports numbers were boosted by extremists who were bussed in, many from regions two or more hours' drive from Gojra. Almas sparked controversy by claiming that at a critical moment in the violence political figures provided weapons, an allegation he set out in a First Information Report (FIR), the preliminary step in criminal proceedings in Pakistan. The claim sparked outrage among the politicians' supporters. Almas and the surviving members of his family received death threats and were taken to a safe-house. While there, Almas told ACN: "My family were killed because of Christ. It is because of our Christian identity that they suffered in this way. I believe our experience – all that we went through – will bear fruit. The blood of my family will bear fruit for the Church in Pakistan."

At a time when legal proceedings against the accused had still to run their course, Almas spoke of his huge difficulties in forgiving his attackers. "When the judge pronounces sentence on them at the end of the trial, then I will forgive." Meantime Almas refused to give in to multi-million rupee bribes intended to persuade him to drop the charges. "I refuse to give in," he said robustly. "Of course they should be forgiven but the people of Pakistan have a right to insist that justice be done."

Philippines

Population	Religions	Christian Population
93 million	Christian 90% Muslim 7% Other 3%	83 million

Under President Gloria Arroyo's government, there has been a significant increase in the number of extra-judicial killings. The victims were often human rights activists and priests, who defended those farming the land. The crimes were concentrated in areas where there has been conflict between the Philippine army and the New People's Army, the armed wing of the Communist Party of the Philippines. However, with the excuse of fighting the rebels, the army has committed abuses of power against the civilian population, killing or imprisoning those who criticise the military.

Many of the problems for the Christian community have occurred on the island of Mindanao. Here there has been an ongoing struggle between the Philippine Army and Islamic extremist groups belonging to the Moro Islamic Liberation Front (MILF) and Abu Sayyaf, a terrorist group linked to al-Qaeda. The extremists have fought to create an independent Islamic state. In 1987 the central government created the "Autonomous Region in Muslim Mindanao" covering much of the island, but the MILF was not happy with the result and clashes with the army have continued. The Christian community has experienced attacks and kidnappings throughout 2009. Those kidnapped included Fr Michael Sinnott, an Irish missionary.

In Mindanao the Bishops-Ulema Conference (BUC), created in 1996 has been working to promote peace. Composed of 24 Catholic bishops, 18 Protestant leaders and 24 ulemas (Muslim scholars), every year it organises "The week for peace in Mindanao". With hostilities between the army and the MILF resuming between April and May 2009, the BUC organised about 300 discussion groups in the various cities on the island, bringing together more than 6,000 people from different social and ethnic groups.

July 2009: A bomb exploded outside the Cathedral of the Immaculate Conception in Cotabato, while Mass was being celebrated by Monsignor Orlando Quevedo. The explosion killed five people, including a three-year-old child, and wounded another 45. Interviewed after the attack, Monsignor Quevedo described it as "not only a crime but also sacrilege".

September 2009: A group of 30 armed men killed Fr Cecilio Lucero (Chairman of the Diocese of Catarman's Human Rights desk of the Social Action Centre), in Northern Samar (an island south-east of Manila). Before his death he had been threatened by the military, whom he had accused of abuses against the population. By that point at least 18 people had been killed. Bishop Emmanuel Trance of Catarman said of Fr Lucero: "Due to his work defending human rights and for having investigated suspicious deaths that took place between January and September 2009, he had turned the soldiers and the communist rebels against himself."

October 2009: A grenade damaged the Cathedral of Our Lady of Mount Carmel in Jolo, the capital of Sulu Province. No one died, but Masses for All Saints and All Souls were cancelled.

October 2009: Fr Michael Sinnott, of the Missionary Society of Saint Columban, was kidnapped at his home in Zamboanga, Mindanao Island, by seven unidentified men. To avoid the Philippine army, the kidnappers made Fr Sinnott walk through the jungle in the province of Lanao del Norte for over a month. In the days that followed the kidnapping, the people of Pagadian and Zamboanga, Catholics and Muslims alike, organised a series of prayer vigils for the release of the priest. Fr Sinnott was released on 12th November 2009 after a joint operation involving the Philippine army.

April 2010: Santa Isabel Cathedral in Basilan Island was hit by a bomb. Less than a third of the structure in Isabela city remained standing. It was widely reported that Abu Sayyaf was responsible for the attack.[269]

June 2010: Three Christian men were beheaded by members of Abu Sayyaf as they were hauling timber in a forest near Maluso town, Basilan Island. Basilan provincial police chief Antonio Mendoza said: "When they are hurt by our offensives, they resort to these atrocities," suggesting the killings were in retaliation for ongoing military and police operations.[270]

December 2010: Eleven people were wounded when a bomb exploded during early morning Christmas Day Mass at the Chapel of the Sacret Heart in Jolo, an island near Mindanao. Muslim leaders condemned the attack which is being blamed on extremists. Islamist groups including Abu Sayyaf and Jemaah Islamiyah were the main suspects.[271]

Russia

Population	Religions	Christian Population
140 million	Christian 60% Agnostic 25% Muslim 10% Other 5%	8 million

Russia has come a long way since the days of the Soviet persecution of religious groups, including Christians but there continue to be areas of concern. Legal regulations for religious organisations have become increasingly stringent. However, despite increased regulation, courts have upheld the constitutional rights of Christian communities. The Good Shepherd Baptist Church in the Black Sea port of Tuapse had its impending liquidation cancelled by a court in May 2008. Officials had stripped it of its registration for failing to file a tax-return, which continues to be a common reason for de-registration.[272]

In 2009 there were particular concerns about an increase in the powers of the Russian Justice Ministry's Expert Council for Conducting State Religious-Studies Analysis, particularly over the choice of Aleksandr Dvorkin as its chair. Dvorkin was dismissed from his post at Moscow State University because of his negative views about religious minorities.[273] The Old Believers (who broke away from the Russian Orthodox Church in the 17th century) called for the abolition of the council, describing it as "a direct threat to the constitutional rights of the citizens of Russia to freedom of confession". They added that it could become "a dangerous catalyst for inter-confessional strife, a prologue to the beginning of struggle against religious dissent, oppression of believers, the restoration of religious censorship and inquisition". Muslims, Catholics and some Orthodox leaders said council members were ignorant about religion.[274]

Tension over the return of former Church property seized after the 1917 Bolshevik Revolution looked set to grow after a controversial law was passed in November 2010. The law was widely criticised by Catholic and other minority groups as favouring the Russian Orthodox Church. It came as Catholic Archbishop Paulo Pezzi of Moscow expressed dismay at the transfer of a former Catholic church in Kaliningrad to the Russian Orthodox Church. Meanwhile, in Lipetsk, Baptists were seeking compensation after a former Russian Orthodox church, transferred to them by Soviet authorities in 1989, was returned to the Orthodox.[275]

However, relations between the Russian Orthodox Church and the Catholic Church have been looking more promising following the election of Metropolitan Kirill as Patriarch in January 2009. Aid to the Church in Need UK Director Neville Kyrke-Smith said: "There are still some suspicions about ecumenism in Russia but Metropolitan Kirill has shown a very balanced attitude in his relations with the Catholic Church."[276] During a visit to the Vatican in May 2010, Archbishop Hilarion Alfeyev of Volokolamsk, chairman of the Department of External Affairs of the Moscow Patriarchate, said Catholics and Orthodox were increasingly seeing themselves as allies instead of competitors. He said the rivalries of the past "must stay there, in the past". Noting the "de-Christianization of our countries" he called for "greater collaboration".[277]

February 2009: Speaking at a local government meeting, the governor of Kaluga Region ordered that land owned by the Word of Life Pentecostal Church be seized by "any" means possible. However, he was unaware that the meeting was being broadcast live via the regional administration's website. The footage was posted on YouTube. Word of Life has complained of bureaucratic harassment ever since being told that its land was required to build a shopping centre.[278]

October 2009: Two Baptist preachers in Kaliningrad were fined after their community "sang psalms and spoke about Christ" in the street. According to police, the Baptists held the event without permission. Aleksandr Legotin, one of the two preachers who were arrested, said that as the Baptists held a service, not a demonstration, the requirement to notify the authorities in advance should not have applied.[279]

November 2009: The Justice Ministry proposed amendments to the 1997 Religion Law and the Administrative Violations Code, imposing tighter controls on religious activity. Andrei Sebentsov, secretary of the government's Commission for Issues Concerning Religious Associations, said the proposed draft was "so clearly against the demands of the constitution that the presidential administration would hardly support it".[280]

November 2009: Fr Daniil Sysoyev was murdered after an unidentified gunman entered his church and shot him twice. The 35-years-old Russian Orthodox priest had a reputation for evangelising the Muslim community.

Kevin O'Flynn of Radio Free Europe Radio Liberty said Fr Sysoyev "would routinely go to the city's construction sites, where many immigrants are employed, and successfully convert as many as 80 people". Fr Sysoyev also warned Christians against marrying Muslims. Before his death, the priest noted on his blog that he had received 14 death threats.[281]

February 2010: Police in Kaluga raided the Sunday morning service of St George's Lutheran congregation. Lutheran Archbishop Iosif Baron was in attendance to ordain Dmitry Martyshenko during the service. Mr Martyshenko said 11 police officers with automatic weapons and police dogs disrupted the service to search for "extremist literature". Officers blocked church doors preventing anyone leaving or entering. The search lasted about an hour. Martyshenko reported hostility to the Lutheran community since it acquired premises in December 2009. He reported several negative articles in local newspapers since the beginning of 2010.[282]

June 2010: Authorities reneged on a five-year agreement allowing members of the Pentecostal Hosanna Church, in the southern Russian republic of Dagestan, to visit prisons. Pastor Artur Suleimanov blamed it on government officials opposed to the Church.[283]

November-December 2010: Latin Catholic Archbishop Paulo Pezzi of Moscow protested against plans to transfer a former Catholic church in Kaliningrad to the Russian Orthodox Patriarchate of Moscow. Archbishop Pezzi criticised the decision, saying that the Catholic Church had spent 20 years trying to win back the former Holy Family Church which was seized after the 1917 Bolshevik Revolution. The controversy came as a law was passed on the restitution of former Church property. Archbishop Pezzi said the law had been "prepared in secret without consulting [non-Orthodox] churches" and other Christian leaders said it was biased against minority groups.[284] In December 2010 the Holy Family Church was handed over to the Russian Orthodox. Without a building of its own, the local Catholic parish has been meeting for services in a temporary structure. [285]

Saudi Arabia

Population	Religions	Christian Population
25 million	Muslim 95%	1 million
	Christian 4%	
	Other 1%	

Saudi Arabia offers no scope for Christians to practise their faith. Religious freedom is not protected under the law and is severely restricted in practice. Public celebrations by non-Islamic religions are banned. Although the government declares the right of non-Muslims to practise their faith privately, reports indicate that the Commission for the Promotion of Virtue and Prevention of Vice and security forces from the Ministry of the Interior continue to raid private religious gatherings and confiscate religious articles.[286]

This climate of oppression has placed huge burdens on the pastoral care of Saudi Arabia's Christian community who number as many as one million. The majority of them come as menial workers from a wide variety of countries including the Philippines and India. Their low social status has made them even more vulnerable.

But there are some glimmers of hope. Soon after becoming king in 2005, Abdullah has initiated what has been described a modernising drive. In February 2009, the king appointed new members to the Council of Grand Ulemas (scholars) who for the first time did not belong to the Hanabite rite that inspires Saudi's official Wahabite tradition, noted for its hard-line, ultra-orthodox vision. These appointments included a new Chief of the Religious Police. Sources have described fewer airport security searches for Bibles and other non-Islamic materials and new measures to stop religious hatred being preached in mosques.

As yet, however, it is not clear if these initiatives will be enough to tackle institutionalised religious intolerance as well as the growth of extremism in society. Reports speak of radicalisation in institutions such as the Army some of whose ranks are said to have links with the likes of Al Qaeda. Some evidence suggests the changes are only intended as window-dressing to allay the concerns of the US and other trade partners. The US State Department continued to list Saudi Arabia as a "country of particular concern" because of persistent religious freedom violations. In a country where Islam is the State religion and *Shari'a* is the basis of the law, Christians are still systematically persecuted. Displaying a cross or other non-Islamic symbol is still strictly forbidden and religious personnel frequently have to travel in secret. The Saudi government has faced criticism for failing to honour its pledge to remove radicalism from school books. Research into Ministry of education official school textbooks (2007-08) discovered statements inciting hatred against the West and in particular Jews who are labelled "apes" and Christians who are "swine…the infidels of the communion of Jesus"[287]. With a Catholic church having been opened in Qatar, Saudi Arabia is now the only Middle East country without a church. Taking all factors into consideration, religious-rights monitors continue to describe Saudi Arabia as one of the top three countries where persecution is worst for Christians.[288]

January 2009: Eritrean pastor Yemane Gebriel was obliged to leave the country for an unknown destination after receiving numerous threats from the religious police. For 10 years Gebriel had led an underground Christian church with over 300 believers.

January 2009: Saudi authorities arrested and imprisoned Hamoud Bin Saleh for describing his conversion to Christianity on his ChristforSaudis blog. He remained under a travel ban after his release at the end of March and was prohibited from blogging.[289]

March 2009: Three Indian Christians found praying together were arrested by the religious police in the eastern province. The police seized religious material from their apartment. The Christians were released a few days later.

October 2009: Indian priest Fr George Joshua gave a lengthy interview about his experience in a Saudi jail and the prayer campaign he established afterwards. In 2006 Fr George was sent to Saudi Arabia to help with Easter preparations for a large number of Indian Catholics working there. At the end of Mass he was arrested and jailed for four days. On return to India, he founded the Christ Army for Saudi Arabia made up of groups who pray and fast for the king, the country's "well-being" and for the cause of religious freedom. Describing a vision he had in jail of "a chalice planted on the map of the Saudi kingdom", he described talking to Indian nurses working there:

"75 percent are Catholics from Kerala. I tell them they should serve their patients with the love of Christ... In Saudi Arabia where Christians and our dear Muslim friends interact so closely... each respecting each other's religion, it gradually builds up fraternal collaboration."[290]

December 2009: Returning home to the Philippines after seven months as a maid to a family in Saudi Arabia, Norma Caldera described her experience as like being in "a prison". She said her colleagues and employees constantly harassed her because of her faith and as a result she was forced to return home five months before the end of her contract. She explained that she was not forbidden to leave her place of work and was denied a bed – and had to sleep on the kitchen floor or in a tent outside the house. She explained: "When I told my employers that I was Catholic and wanted to die a Catholic, the first thing they did was lower my salary." She was banned from attending Mass and was forced to fast during Ramadan. She went on: "Every day I got up early to pray and every time my colleagues and employers saw me they began to insult and mock me because of my Christian faith. I lived through this experience, praying and having faith in God. I was willing to make this sacrifice to be able to pay for my two daughters' education."[291]

August 2010: A man purporting to be an Al-Qaeda leader ordered supporters in the Saudi army to topple the Saudi monarchy for helping the US to fight fellow Muslims in Afghanistan, Iraq and elsewhere and called for the country's Christians to be killed. The voice message was carried on a website with Al-Qaeda sympathies. As well as calling for "arms to be taken up against Israel," the speaker, identified as Saeed al-Shihri, said, "You who work as guards for tyrants, princes, ministers or complexes where Christians live... seek help from Allah to kill them."[292]

September: A Filipino nurse working at Kharja Hospital, near Riyadh, died after being raped and left for dead in the desert by her assailants.[293]

October 2010: Saudi authorities conditionally released 12 Filipino Catholics working in the country accused of proselytising into the custody of their employers. The Philippines embassy in Saudi Arabia was reported to be negotiating with the authorities for their repatriation. The Saudi religious police arrested them on 1st October 2009 for taking part in a Mass celebrated by a French priest. The fate of 150 other foreign Catholics arrested with them is unknown.[294]

Sri Lanka

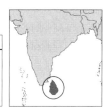

Population	Religions	Christian Pop.
20 million	Buddhist 70% Muslim 8% Christian 8% Hindu 7%, Other 0.5%	1.6 million

The sudden escalation of violence between Sri Lanka's national army and the Liberation Tigers of Tamil Eelam resulted in victory for the government forces in May 2009. Amid reports of a deepening humanitarian crisis, Church leaders became increasingly alarmed and mounted emergency aid operations. These programmes concentrated on those in the worst-affected areas in the north and the east where the government would eventually wipe out the Tamil military presence. In March 2009, as the end of the conflict approached, Catholic Bishop Thomas Savundaranayagam of Jaffna wrote to President Mahinda Rajapaksa warning that more than 100,000 people faced "total annihilation" – unless immediate evacuation got under way.[295] Following the conflict, many of the 300,000 made homeless by the conflict found themselves in Internal Displacement Camps. News reports suggested that conditions in the military-run camps were extremely poor, access to the camps by non-government agencies was severely limited and those in them were not allowed to leave in the months following the end of the conflict. By late 2010, most had returned to rebuild their homes and livelihoods, but there were still more than 25,000 in displacement camps whose freedom of movement was tightly controlled. Disaster emergency monitoring teams reported that there were another 200,000 internally-displaced people in the region who had fled their homes in the period before 2006 during sporadic civil conflicts with the Tamil Tigers.[296]

From late 2008 onwards, there were relatively few reports of anti-Christian violence, but cases increased after the war ended. This was associated with the rise of Sinhalese Buddhist nationalism, which sees Sri Lankan identity as inextricably linked with Sinhalese ethnicity and Theravada Buddhist culture. Sinhalese Buddhist nationalism has caused religious tensions between Buddhists and various religious minorities, including Christians. Christians were accused of converting Buddhists by unethical means, which led to violence and discrimination at a local level.[297] A peak was reported by the National Christian Evangelical Alliance of Sri Lanka between June and August 2009 when attacks on Christians were reported in

Puttlam, Gampaha and Kurunegala districts in western Sri Lanka, central Polonnaruwa district, Mannar district in the north and Matara district in the south.[298] However, reports of violence declined in 2010.

The passage of "A Bill on Prohibition of Forcible Conversions of Religion" – a private members bill sponsored by political party Jathika Hela Urumaya – continued to be of concern to Christians. The bill was backed by the All Ceylon Buddhist Congress which, in January 2009, claimed there was a plot to undermine Buddhism in the country. They alleged that Christian groups were not only engaged in unethical conversions, but were supporting terrorism.[299]

The bill sought to criminalize any attempt to convert a person from one religion to another by force, fraud or allurement. Those found guilty could be imprisoned for up to seven years and/or fined up to 500,000 rupees. Following the first reading of the bill in Parliament in August 2004, 22 petitions were filed in the Supreme Court challenging the validity of the draft legislation. Controversially the bill included articles setting out regulations for religious conversions to be reported to the authorities with a set of punishments for failure to do so. However, the Supreme Court ruled that this was unconstitutional and the articles concerned were dropped from the bill.[300]

Ahead of another reading of the bill, the Catholic Bishops' Conference of Sri Lanka proclaimed a national day of fasting, abstinence, and prayer for 3rd April 2009.[301] The National Christian Evangelical Alliance of Sri Lanka declared: "It is our gravest concern that this bill will grant legal sanction for the harassment of religious communities or individuals and offer convenient tools of harassment for settling personal disputes and grudges, totally unrelated to acts of alleged 'forced' conversion." Christians also expressed concern that key sections of the draft bill were open to subjective interpretations that could make it illegal for faith-based organisations to carry out social or welfare support work.[302]

December 2008: Sri Lanka Air Force bombers destroyed a Christian centre for orphaned and disabled girls close to the A9 highway in Ki'linochchi town, at 4.30pm on Christmas day. The girls had been moved to a different building and no one was injured in the attack. The area was in the designated safe zone and administrators of the centre, run by the Jaffna Catholic diocese, said they are did not know why they were targeted.[303]

January 2009: After being refused formal permission to visit parts of Vanni region affected by fighting, Bishop Thomas Savundaranayagam, travelled incognito to see the situation for himself and entrust ACN aid for the needy to local clergy.[304]

February 2009: Bishop Savundaranayagam and Apostolic Nuncio Mario Zenari met Sri Lankan President Mahinda Rajapaksa and called for a cessation of violence and immediate relief aid for thousands of internal refugees.[305]

March 2009: Bishop Savundaranayagam wrote to President Mahinda Rajapaksa, pleading on behalf of 100,000 people trapped in a narrow, seven-mile-long 'safe zone' in the coastal district of Mulaithivu in the north-east of the country, as government and rebel forces are preparing for "the final battle". He stressed that the people in the safe zone faced a humanitarian crisis.[306]

April 2009: Four Buddhist extremists approached the home of Protestant Pastor Pradeep Kumara in Weeraketiya, Hambanthota district, calling for him to come out and threatening to kill him. At the time the pastor's wife was at home with their two children. She phoned him immediately but by the time he returned, the men had left. Half an hour later he received phone calls threatening to kill him if he did not leave the village by the following morning. Later one of the men returned to the house and shouted threats. Police arrived and arrested the instigator but released him the following day. Subsequently the man instigated a petition against the church, and protestors warned the Kumaras' landlord they would destroy the house if he did not evict the family by the end of the month. Fearing violence, Kumara cancelled Good Friday and Easter Sunday services and moved his children out of the village.[307]

April 2009: On Palm Sunday, a group of men broke into the 150-year-old Pepiliyana Methodist Church in Colombo. "They removed everything, including valuable musical instruments, a computer, Bibles, hymn books and all the church records," said the Rev Surangika Fernando. The church enjoyed good relations with other villagers, and the Rev Fernando said the break-in was more than a simple robbery as baptism and marriage records were stolen.[308]

April 2009: Anti-Christian mobs in Vakarai, eastern Batticaloa district, intimidated church members gathering for several services during Holy Week. "What can we do?" Pastor Kanagalingam Muraleetharan said. "The authorities and the police say we have the right to worship, but the reality is that people are threatened."[309]

June 2009: A Foursquare Gospel pastor from Polonnaruwa district was stopped by three masked men riding motorcycles who attacked him with knives. The assailants shouted, "This is your last day! If we let you live, you will convert the whole town!" The pastor sustained severe cuts to his arms as he warded off blows. Police investigated the incident.[310]

June 2009: In Thalvapadu village, Mannar district, a mob of about 300 people forcibly entered a newly constructed Protestant church as it was being consecrated. The mob demolished the building.[311]

June 2009: A mob of more than 100 people, including Buddhist monks, surrounded the home of the female pastor of a Foursquare Gospel church in Puttlam district. The pastor's 13-year-old daughter was at home when the mob broke in, shouting insults and destroying furniture. The pastor and her husband heard of the attack and went to get police help, but the mob had left by the time officers arrived. On her way to give a police statement the following month, protestors surrounded her, spat at her and tried to stop her entering the station. Later the pastor was pressured to sign a document agreeing not hold services – except for those confined to members of her family.[312]

June 2009: Four priests of the diocese of Jaffna and two Oblate Missionaries of Mary Immaculate were imprisoned and kept in secret solitary confinement in camps for internally displaced persons. They had been helping the Tamil people during the war until the end of the military campaign.[313]

June 2009: Bishop Savundaranayagam of Jaffna told how one priest died of "exhaustion" ministering to people in the camps, and praised others for their work among the afflicted. He said there were now more than 200,000 refugees and 18 parishes in Kilinochy and Mullaitivu were now "totally kaput". He wrote: "I saw parishes falling one after the other. I have no

116

access to those places now – no people, no parishes, no priests, no churches. Some of my priests were staying till the last with the people and were rescued by the Army. They are still in the refugee camps."[314]

July 2009: Seven men wielding swords attacked caretaker Akila Dias and three other members of the Vineyard Community Church in Markandura village, Kurunegala district. Dias and others received emergency care at a local hospital before being transferred to a larger hospital. This was the latest in a long line of attacks. One of the attackers had assaulted the church pastor and another worker with a machete in March, and on 29th June the church premises were smeared with human faeces. On the night of 12th July, attackers tore tiles off the church's roof.[315]

July 2009: A mob razed an Assemblies of God church in Norachcholai, Puttlam district by fire. The pastor received frantic calls from neighbours around 8.45pm reporting that the building was ablaze. This follows an arson attack in July 2008 that destroyed the original church building.[316]

July 2009: In Gampaha district, a mob destroyed the partially built home of Sanjana Kumara, a Christian resident of Obawatte village. On receiving a phone call from a friend, Kumara returned home to find the house's supporting pillars pulled down. The actions are believed to be reprisals for him inviting his minister to bless the construction. During the blessing about 30 people entered the house threatening to kill Kumara and accused him of building a church on the site. Kumara also discovered his storage had been broken into. Tools had been stolen and a Buddhist blessing painted on the walls.[317]

July 2009: The pastor of a Foursquare Gospel church and his wife were harangued by a 50-strong mob when he went to visit a church member in Radawana village, Gampaha district. They mob shouted they would not tolerate any further Christian activity in the village. They prevented the couple from leaving the house, hit the pastor with a rod, and threw a bucket of cow dung at him. The disturbance continued for two hours before police finally answered repeated requests for assistance and arrived at the house, arresting three people.[318]

August 2009: The National Christian Evangelical Alliance of Sri Lanka reported that attacks on Christians increased drastically following the government troop's defeat of Tamil separatists in May.[319]

September 2009: Our Lady, Rosa Mystica Church in Crooswatta, near Kotugoda, was attacked by Buddhists as Sunday Mass was finishing. Fr Jude Lakshman, said: "A mob of about a thousand people with sticks, swords and stones stormed the church when I and my parishioners were still inside... They smashed statues, the altar and chairs. They destroyed everything." The mob also set cars outside on fire and attacked worshippers. The church had previously been targeted by Buddhist extremists in 2006 and 2007, who objected to a church being built near to a Buddhist monastery. This lead to construction being temporarily halted, but in 2008 the Supreme Court gave the go ahead for work to continue.[320]

November 2009: A mob of more than 200 people attacking the Jesus-Never-Fails Prayer Centre in Colombo District was captured on video. The attackers were by members of a protest march led by members of political party Jathika Hela Urumaya and Buddhist monks. Protestors damaged the building's exterior, windows, air conditioning units and main gates.[321]

May 2010: Archbishop Joseph Spiteri, Apostolic Nuncio in Sri Lanka, visited the north and east of the island. He carried out a pastoral visitation to parishes, seminaries, orphanages and camps for the displaced in Jaffna, Trincomalee, Batticaloa and Mannar. The nuncio said he was "satisfied by the Church's commitment to the victims of war."[322]

July 2010: Archbishop Ranjith of Colombo told Sri Lanka's Education Minister Bandula Gunawardana that several current history and geography textbooks contained defamatory remarks against the Pope, Catholics and the Church. The archbishop said, "This is an attempt to create disharmony among the religious communities...It is an attempt to instil very insulting and defamatory concepts in the minds of the students and also to discredit the government." The Minister promised to investigate following their meeting.[323]

Sudan

Population	Religions	Christian Population
38 million	Muslim 70% Christian 15% Local religions 12% Others 3%	5.5 million

The struggle to find a long-term political solution to the decades-long dispute between Muslim north Sudan and the largely Christian communities in the south reached a climax with the referendum of January 2011. Voters were facing the choice of Sudan remaining a united country or the south seceding to become a separate nation. Overshadowing the political debate throughout this period was the fear that, if the referendum were to fail, the country would return to full-scale conflict. About 2.5 million people died in the 1983-2005 civil war, which ended with a six-year interim power-sharing deal between the Government of National Unity in the north and the former rebels – the Sudanese People's Liberation Movement (SPLM) – in the south. Christians across Sudan voiced concerns that President Omar al-Bashir's regime remained as committed to Islamist domination of the south as it did at the height of the war. Bashir certainly had less reason to compromise. The national elections of 2009 – the first for more than 20 years – returned him to power with a strong majority. Nor did Bashir seem likely to concede after a robust response in March 2009, when he was indicted for war crimes in Darfur by the International Criminal Court in The Hague.

As 2011 dawned, the political process seemed to be in serious trouble amid reports that referendum preparations had stalled and that troops and armaments were massing in border regions. The criticism also applied to the SPLM, who were accused of massive corruption, incompetence and a lack of faith in the political process. The lack of investment in the war-decimated South Sudan meant that relatively few Christians returned from the north, where they had lived for decades, following displacement brought about by the civil war. Bishop Eduardo Hiiboro Kussala, guest-of-honour at ACN events in London and Scotland, was one of a number of bishops, who in autumn 2010 travelled to the West to call on world powers to intervene in Sudan to prevent catastrophe.

Against this fraught political backdrop, Christians continued to suffer atrocities with churches being attacked. There was stunted growth in the war-decimated south. The most shocking reported act of violence took place in Ezo in the extreme south in the late summer of 2009. Christians stumbled upon the remains of fellow Christians nailed to pieces of wood. They described it as resembling a mock crucifixion scene. The dead were made up of people abducted during a church service by the Lord's Resistance Army (LRA), a rebel movement. Meanwhile in the north, the greater freedoms offered to Christians in a region under *Shari'a* law seemed in doubt, especially after Sudan's Cardinal Zubeir Wako of Khartoum was the target of an assassination attempt in October 2010. In a region heavily affected by Islamism, Christian schools were considered by bishops to be a top priority, especially in the context of ongoing social, educational and job discrimination. Christian leaders cited educational requirements as exacerbating problems in the relationship between the Muslim majority and the Christian minority and as further marginalising the place of Christianity in northern society.[324]

March 2009: Authorities in Chat, in the Nuba Mountains, led an attack against two Christian places of worship, both of which were destroyed. The destruction of the two Protestant churches was apparently intended as retaliation after the International Criminal Court in The Hague indicted Sudanese President Omar al-Bashir for war crimes. The attacks in Chat followed a series of violent acts against churches elsewhere in the country, including a bomb attack on the Episcopalian Church of Shatt Mazarik on 7th March 2009. Two weeks later, there was an attack on the Catholic church in Shatt Dammam. According to local Christians, the police from the nearby town of Kadugli did not launch any investigation into the crimes.

April 2009: A female convert to Christianity suffered violence at the hands of her husband and was imprisoned for three days. Halima Bubkier, 35, a mother of three, explained how she embraced Christianity after seeing a film about Jesus and her husband initially allowed her to attend church services. But Muslim hardliners in Sinarr town, near Khartoum, were shocked to discover her conversion and banned her husband from attending communal evening meals during Ramadan. Mrs Bubkier said her husband turned on her and threw an armchair at her, injuring her back. She alleges he then removed all his belongings from their home and set it on fire. The

120

couple's two older children, aged six and eight, stayed with their father, while she took the youngest, aged just two. Mrs Bubkier tried to take refuge with her older brother, Nur Bubkier, but when he discovered her conversion he beat her, and threatened her with a knife. She received an interim jail sentence on charges of 'disrespecting Islam'. However, shortly before she was due to appear before a judge, a Coptic priest intervened, pointing out to police that the law forbids people being jailed because of their religion. She was then freed.[325]

July-October 2009: Lubna Ahmed Hussein, a journalist and former UN worker, refused to pay a US$150 (£100, €120) fine for wearing trousers in public and began a campaign to give rights to women. She was among a group of 13 women arrested in a Khartoum restaurant for inappropriate clothing. 10 of the women pleaded guilty and were flogged (20 lashes). Ms Hussein was jailed after refusing to pay the fine. She was released after 24 hours, after Sudan's journalists' union raised the money. Supporters of Ms Hussein's campaign quoted police statistics for 2008 showing that 42,000 women in Khartoum – many living in Christian enclaves – were detained by security forces and a number of them were flogged. Ms Hussein resigned her position at the UN so she could publicise her case.[326]

August-September 2009: Rebel soldiers burst into Our Lady Queen of Peace Catholic Church, Ezo town during a prayer vigil. They desecrated the church and abducted 17 faithful, mostly in their teens and 20s. Shortly after the attack one of those abducted was found dead. He had been tied to a tree and mutilated. Three others returned to safety the following day, leaving 13 still missing. The attack, apparently carried out by the LRA, took place close to Sudan's border with the Central African Republic and the Democratic Republic of Congo. The LRA are also blamed for another attack that took place the following day in the nearby town of Nzara. There, six people were ambushed in a forest and killed after being nailed to pieces of wood fastened to the ground. Those who discovered the bodies several days later likened it to a grotesque crucifixion scene. In response, Bishop Eduardo Hiiboro Kussala of Tombura-Yambio organised a three-day prayer event involving Christians of all denominations from across Western Equatoria State. At the event's climax, 20,000 people walked barefoot for more than two miles (3 km) wearing sackcloth and ashes. The march was also a protest at the government's failure to increase security in the region.[327]

October 2010: A man with a dagger ran towards Cardinal Gabriel Zubeir Wako, Archbishop of Khartoum, during a Mass in the Comboni Play Ground in the city. Before he reached the cardinal, the man was intercepted by the prelate's Master of Ceremonies, Barnaba Matnec Anei, who handed him over to police. The man, who was identified as Hamdan Mohamed Abdurrahman, may have entered the venue very early, before security staff arrived to check people before the service. It was not clear whether Mr Abdurrahman was acting alone. Sudan's Bishop Eduardo Hiiboro Kussala told ACN: "For those with extreme views, it would of course be a good thing to kill a leader like the cardinal. He has been targeted many times but he has always maintained a very strong faith."[328]

October 2010: Bishop Eduardo Hiiboro Kussala of Tombura-Yambio, South Sudan, highlighted concerns about the country's security situation in the run-up to the referendum on possible secession of South Sudan. Speaking at Aid to the Church in Need's annual Westminster Event, he outlined fears of a return to war amid reports of disagreement over the boundary between north and South Sudan and a build-up of weapons and military in border regions. He said Christians in the north had been labelled "cockroaches". He said Christians in and around Khartoum had been warned of acts of violence and persecution if they fail to vote for national unity. He concluded by calling on the international community to intervene to avoid conflict. He said: "If the referendum goes well, it will bring peace to a country which has suffered almost five decades of brutal civil war. If however the referendum does not deliver a credible result, then Sudan will descend into violence and instability which will affect the whole region."

December 2010: Cardinal Keith O'Brien, Archbishop of St Andrews and Edinburgh, wrote to UK Foreign Secretary William Hague warning of the "potential for widespread violence" in southern Sudan ahead of the referendum. The cardinal called for UN-led initiatives to ensure proper conduct in the voting. Noting the "extreme lack of progress in preparation for the referendum", the cardinal urged Mr Hague "to do everything you can to prevent the outbreak of further conflict in southern Sudan."[329]

January 2011: Voters went to the polls in the long-awaited referendum. Latest reports suggested the vote had passed the threshold needed to validate the ballot. Auxiliary Bishop Daniel Adwok of Khartoum told ACN: "The referendum has been conducted in a peaceful atmosphere."

Profile: Bishop Akio Johnson of Torit, Sudan

"Why did you come and teach people about God? And where is God anyway?" Before the young Christian man had a chance to answer, he heard the sound of gunshot. But Akio Johnson did not die – nor indeed was he injured. He looked over and there was his friend, John, the chief catechist of this village of Oraju, writhing in agony. Suddenly, the attacker swung his gun towards Akio. In a split second, Akio charged towards him, kicked the gun from his hands and grabbed it. The man fled the scene and Akio was left tending to the catechist whose life slipped away in his hands.

This is one of a host of near-death experiences Bishop Akio Johnson recounts. The energetic 52-year-old with a ready smile used to be known as "the Bishop with nine lives" before his brushes with mortality reached double figures. Meeting ACN staff during a project and fact-finding trip to Sudan in July 2009, he pointed to a scar and a crevice in his forehead and behind his ear – the distinctive marks of one lucky escape. He told his dramatic story in ramshackle farm buildings which make up his temporary home in the centre of Torit, where he is bishop. This region of Western Equatoria, not far from the border with Uganda, bore the brunt of the country's civil war between 1983 and 2005. More than 2.5 million people lost their lives during Africa's longest-running civil conflict waged between the Islamist regime in Khartoum and the Christian/Animist rebels in the south. Akio Johnson's own home in the Torit area was targeted repeatedly. At one point, it was bombed more than 70 times within three weeks. During this period of the 1990s, this mostly Catholic region was forcibly Islamised. Road signs were changed to Arabic and *Shari'a* law was enforced. Hundreds of youngsters were taken to Khartoum, where they were trained as child soldiers and subjected to Islamist brain-washing.

Akio Johnson suffered alongside his people. Ordained a priest of Torit diocese in 1988, he was created auxiliary Bishop of Torit in 1999. Recalling those dark days, Bishop Akio says: "The people's anger welled up over many years and was constantly renewed by new experiences of pain and anguish."

Assisting Bishop Paride Taban, an iconic bearded figure who led Torit diocese through the time of war, Akio Johnson said that the key to the Church's pastoral approach was "to stay with the people through thick and thin". The priests often travelled at night, behind enemy lines, ministering to the people and giving them the sacraments.

Sudan is haunted by its past but now must reckon with a future which is far from clear. Looking ahead, the creation of a new country of South Sudan was for many Sudanese a long-cherished dream that all but perished during the civil war. For the Church meantime, the breathing space provided by 2005's Comprehensive Peace Agreement has at last given Bishop Akio the chance to start building for the future.

But where to begin? One of the first people we met on our arrival in Torit was Bishop Akio's vicar general, Fr Joseph Okello, himself a veteran of the war years. Pointing to a sorry collection of derelict buildings behind a forbidding barbed wire fence, he said: "The Bishop has no cathedral, no offices, very few churches. He doesn't even have a house of his own to live in – everywhere is damaged and destroyed. It is very difficult for us."

But stepping into view with a beaming smile, Bishop Akio welcomed us, saying: "It is true: there are a lot of challenges to face but we are not down-hearted. We know that God always stays with his people."

In any case, buildings are not his priority. After taking over from Bishop Paride Taban as the Bishop of Torit in 2007, Bishop Akio had already made it plain that his priorities are faith formation, Catholic education and income generation projects such as small farms. He said: "My most urgent priority is the spiritual renewal of people. During the time of war, people were Christian because they were against the oppressors. I want people to be Christian through conviction."

And in that task, the energetic bishop is determined to take the lead. As dusk fell over this tragic land, he took us to the nearby St Teresa's School. Standing on a tree stump, Bishop Akio began singing in a sweet, melodic voice. Then came the chorus: "Jesus number one, Jesus number one". The children repeated the refrain. It was a timely reminder that Sudan's future could yet be very different from its all too tragic past.

124

Turkey

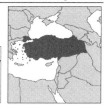

Population	Religions	Christian Population
75 million	Muslim 97% Christian 0.3% Other 2.7%	150,000

Growing concerns about the rise of extremism in Turkey came to a head on 4th June 2010 when Bishop Luigi Padovese, president of the country's Catholic Bishops' Conference, was killed in a bloody attack that shocked the world. Reports initially stated that the assassin was a manic depressive but evidence later emerged linking the killing to influential subversive groups determined to safeguard the country's Islamic identity and prevent Turkey's entry into the EU.[330] Continuing reports of human rights abuses are blamed for the ongoing decline of the country's dwindling Christian community. Many Christians have sought a new life away from the periodic attacks on the Church in the media, the workplace and in public institutions such as schools and places of worship. There are ongoing reports of violence and intimidation especially against alleged missionary activity.

Reports show that Christians in Turkey do not feel the government provides sufficient protection for minorities in spite of statements concerning freedom of religion and belief found in Turkish Criminal Law and the Turkish Constitution. EU negotiation talks and accession requirements led to new religious freedom legislation. At a meeting with Christian leaders in August 2009, Prime Minister Tayyip Erdoğan said "democratic reforms" would ensure the rights of religious minorities. But doubts persist, especially with fresh reports showing that mob attacks against Christians have continued to rise.[331]

One ray of hope for Christians in Turkey came in July 2009 when the authorities raised the possibility of reopening the Halki Greek Orthodox seminary, which would allow the country to train Christian leaders. The seminary had been closed since 1971.[332] In late 2010 at an international conference on religious freedom in Turkey it was announced that the seminary was still closed. However other hopes of change were realised. After a struggle dating back more than 10 years, the Bukukada Orphanage, reportedly one of the largest wooden buildings in the world, was returned to Bartholomew I's Greek Orthodox Patriarchate in November 2010.

125

November 2009: A news agency investigating Turkey uncovered serious violations of international human rights especially concerning religious freedom. Forum 18 found that despite persistent requests the government had not given legal recognition to various religious communities. Also there had been many religiously motivated attacks and threats, especially against Christians. Reports show that although there were fewer instances of religious intolerance in the mainstream media, it was still prevalent in local and nationalist newspapers and websites. The trial of those accused of the 2007 murder of three Protestants in Malatya stalled and there was similarly little or no progress in a number of long-standing property disputes involving Churches including the Greek Orthodox, the Syrian Orthodox and Protestants.[333].

June 2010: Bishop Luigi Padovese of Iskenderun, Anatolia, and President of the Catholic Bishops' Conference of Turkey was killed by his driver and aide, Murat Altun. The murder, on 3rd June 2010, took place at the bishop's house in Iskenderun. An autopsy showed that the bishop, 63, had been beheaded and had received multiple stab wounds to the chest. At the time, Vatican and Turkish government officials stated that the killing was motivated by "personal reasons" amid reports indicating that 26-year-old Altun was suffering from mental illness. However, the autopsy indicated the hallmarks of an Islamic ritual killing and according to first-hand testimonies, Altun had shouted "Allah Akbar. I have killed the great Satan." Mgr Ruggero Franceschini, Archbishop of Izmir, who was named administrator (caretaker) of Mgr Padovese's diocese, stated that the killing was premeditated and that it was the work of "religious fanatics and ultra-nationalists". Aid to the Church in Need projects staff who worked closely with Bishop Padovese described him as "a man of God, a person of great faith, dedicated to helping the Christian faithful withstand a situation of great difficulty".[334]

November 2010: A number of government committees announced proposals for schools' reform. It led many to fear the introduction of Islamic ideology into the education system in a move bound to have negative repercussions for Christians and other minorities. Among the proposals, which must be approved by Turkey's General Council, are plans to allow students to attend religious vocational schools (*iman-hatin*), a scheme to give Islam more dominance in the curriculum and an initiative to divide classes according to gender.[335]

Venezuela

Population	Religions	Christian Population
29 million	Christian 98% Other 2%	28 million

The worsening human rights situation in Venezuela deteriorated still further with reports that President Hugo Chavez's regime was considering plans to confiscate churches, schools and other religious buildings. Noting that the vast majority of Venezuelans were at least nominally Catholic, a source close to the Venezuelan bishops told Aid to the Church in Need staff that elements in the government were intent on "eliminating the work of the Church".[336] One local government official announced a scheme to expropriate Church-run schools, stating the need to protect buildings of national importance. When a new education law was introduced, Venezuelan Cardinal Jorge Urosa Savino said the legislation "takes out religion" from schools, "a right which is in the constitution".[337] Education chiefs were warned that failure to comply could result in schools being shut down and teachers banned from the classroom for up to 10 years.

As President Chavez has pushed ahead with his socialist agenda, apparently inspired by Fidel Castro's Cuba, the Church has increasingly angered the regime by speaking out against human rights abuses, which have been verified by other sources both within and outside the country. Once again placing Venezuela on its 'observation list', the US State Department lamented the "politicisation of the judiciary and official harassment of the political opposition".[338] The report listed abuses including unlawful killings, summary executions of criminal suspects, arbitrary arrests and detention, infringement of citizens' privacy rights by security forces as well as government closure of radio and television stations.

Chavez vowed to "radicalise" his Socialist revolution even further, despite a very narrow victory for his party in September 2010's national assembly elections. The vote, which denied the president an absolute majority in the chamber, fanned his opponents' hopes of unseating him in the 2012 presidential elections.[339] Prospects for improved Church-state relations remain slim. (The government once accused the Catholic Church of conspiring with the USA against the regime.) The possibility of a change

127

for the better looks improbable, especially after the approval of a constitutional referendum eliminating fixed terms for elected officials.

January 2009: Members of 'La Piedrita' launched teargas at the house of the Apostolic Nuncio, the sixth attack in two years. The attackers left pamphlets denouncing priests who had criticised the government. It is believed that the attack was a result of the fact that the Nunciature had granted asylum to members of the opposition as well as a student activist.

June 2009: The President of the Catholic Bishops' Conference of Venezuela, Archbishop Ubaldo Santana, said the political agenda of President Chavez had provoked a "growing political polarisation, increased violence, insecurity and hatred and seriously jeopardised a peaceful democratic society". The archbishop made his comments during the Venezuelan bishops' *ad limina* visit to Rome to meet Pope Benedict XVI. Defending the Church's outspoken criticism of the Chavez regime, Archbishop Santana said: "We have reminded leaders and citizens [in Venezuela] of the fundamental principles of the Church's social doctrine. We have defended the poorest among us and we have always sought out the common good and peaceful democratic coexistence."[340]

August 2009: Cardinal Jorge Urosa Savino, Archbishop of Caracas, warned that an education bill signed into law by President Chavez would remove religious education from the country's schools. Denouncing the law as unconstitutional, the cardinal and other critics spoke out against a particular clause stating that education in both private and state schools was required to have "a lay character... in all circumstances". The cardinal said the new law "does not take God out of the schools but takes out religion, a right which is in the constitution". The cardinal said the law represented a major problem for the Catholic Church since it runs a large number of elementary and high schools. Jesuit Father Luis Ugalde, rector of the Andres Bello Catholic University in Caracas, said the education law was very similar to "the Cuban model". In recent years, students of private and state universities have emerged as opposition leaders to Chavez's policies and students have staged violent protests against the proposed legislation.[341]

September 2009: "The Caracas Newspaper" published an article entitled "The Cardinal's administrative mistake" giving details of an email allegedly from Cardinal Urosa apparently endorsing class divisions in schools. The cardinal denied writing the email.

November 2009: When a local government leader announced plans to confiscate various Church-run schools, a source close to the Venezuelan bishops told Aid to the Church in Need that Catholic representatives "fear that this may be the first step in a general confiscation programme that would affect Church properties throughout the country".

May 2010: Pictures of weapons of war were daubed on images of Jesus Christ and Our Lady of Coromoto in Caracas. Mgr Baltazar Porras, Vice President of the Catholic Bishops' Conference, described the acts as "a way of sowing hatred and death" among the people.

July 2010: Cardinal Urosa issued a statement denouncing "the danger that is threatening our beloved homeland". He accused the Chavez government of trying to install a Marxist-Socialist regime through "unconstitutional" and "illegal" methods which knowingly go against the will of the people. He wrote: "Going beyond the national constitution, President Hugo Chavez and his government want to lead the country on the path to Marxist Socialism which monopolises all spaces, is totalitarian and leads to a dictatorship, not of the proletariat, but of the leadership that governs."[342]

July 2010: President Chavez offended Catholics by remarks he made on national television about the Pope and the country's Catholic bishops. Describing the Pope, the President said: "He is not an ambassador of Christ. Christ is in the people." He went on: "Christ doesn't need any ambassadors," adding that Venezuela's relationship with the Holy See "should be reviewed". Describing Cardinal Urosa, he said: "I called you a 'Neanderthal'. Let me say it again: 'Neanderthal' ". He also called the Venezuelan bishops "a bunch of cavemen".[343]

October 2010: Catholic leaders welcomed the results of the 26th September National Assembly elections that reduced the majority of President Hugo Chavez, saying the chamber was now "democratic" and no longer "fearful".[344]

Vietnam

Population	Religions	Christian Population
88 million	None 80% Buddhist 10% Christian 7% Other 23 %	6.5 million

Over the last few years both the United States and the Holy See have acknowledged some improvements in the situation concerning religious freedom in the country. The government has sanctioned the construction of churches and the training of priests and religious and has permitted the expansion of religious charitable activities. In December 2009 Vietnamese President Nguyên Minh Triêt met Benedict XVI, the first visit of its kind by the head of a communist country.[345] Vietnam and the Holy See subsequently agreed to a Vatican appointment of a non-resident representative as a first step toward the establishment of full diplomatic relations.

However, there continue to be serious concerns about human rights and religious freedom. While the US State Department removed Vietnam from its list of "countries of particular concern" over religious freedom in November 2006, there were calls to return it to the list in 2010. An emergency session of Tom Lantos Human Rights Commission (which promotes Human Rights in the US House of Representatives) highlighted incidents such as the disruption of a Catholic funeral in Con Dau by riot police in May 2010 and called on the US administration to formally recognise Vietnam's human rights abuses.[346]

Incidents of persecution against Christians have continued. Some Christian groups reported government harassment and excessive use of force. A number of churches claimed government forces had either sanctioned or actually taken part in violence against them. Some Protestant groups reported undue delays in obtaining government registration, while others reported being verbally abused. After five years, the government had still to approve a translation of the Bible into an important local language.[347] A particular problem has been the requisitioning of land, but reports suggested this had more to do with rising land prices than anti-Christian sentiment.

The case of Tam Toa Church, in Vinh diocese, south of the capital, Hanoi, illustrates many of the problems. During the Vietnam War, the historic church was bombed by US planes, leaving only the façade and the tower standing. Parishioners were too poor to rebuild the structure, but continued to hold religious services there. In 1996, the People's Committee of Quang Binh Province confiscated the property to turn it into "memorial site". In July 2009, rumours began circulating that it was due for demolition so a tourist resort could be built. During a protest against the plans, plainclothes police and party activists attacked Catholic worshippers, beating men, women and children. Seven Catholics were arrested. Two priests, Fathers Paul Nguyen Dinh Phu and Peter Nguyen The Binh, ended up in Dong Hoi Hospital, the first with broken ribs and head wounds, the second in a coma. General Hoang Cong Tu, from the Public Security Ministry, denied that any violence had been used against the priests. The diocese responded by posting online pictures showing the priests and the wounds. General Tu announced that the seven Catholics accused of "disorderly conduct" would be put on trial. A few weeks later bulldozers demolished what was left of the church, leaving only the tower standing.

Despite all these difficulties, reports have shown the Catholic Church to be growing quickly. In Ho Chi Minh City (formerly Saigon) 2,000 young people were baptised at the Easter vigil in 2009.[348] Seminarians have grown in number by up to 50 percent and now total nearly 1,500.[349] Reports suggest Protestantism is also growing rapidly in the country, although Protestants outside of the state-sanctioned Evangelical Church of Vietnam frequently experience difficulties, particularly small independent house churches. However, both the Baptist and Mennonite communities were granted state recognition in 2007. Reports state that the Baptists have attracted more than 18,400 members since they were established in the country in 1989.[350]

January 2009: Prime Minister Nguyen Tan Dung issued a directive declaring that none of the 2,250 properties seized from the Vietnamese Church (before 1st July 1991) would be returned. He said Christians who might be tempted to organise a protest against government action would be severely punished for causing "social disorder".

January 2009: An Appeal Court in Hanoi heard an application filed by eight members of the Thai Ha Parish, in Hanoi, against their conviction for "disorderly conduct" and "damaging state property". The defendants were part of a crowd of thousands who protested against a decision to take land from their church. Defence attorneys were prevented from submitting any evidence. Despite the defendants pleading not guilty, state media claimed the accused "sincerely admitted their guilt and begged for the government's mercy".

February 2009: In Son La province, in the country's northwest region on the border with Laos, local authorities allegedly led a campaign to eradicate Christianity. They promoted a revival in the country's ancient pagan practices and beliefs. Families that resisted were denied welfare benefits and were shunned by fellow villagers.

February 2009: A delegation from the Holy See was warmly welcomed by Hanoi Catholics. Mgr Pietro Parolin, Undersecretary of State, who led the Vatican delegation, acknowledged that the situation had improved over recent years. But he also "took notice" – a phrase that indicates the absence of complete agreement – of the explanations given by Deputy Foreign Minister Nguyen Quoc Cuong regarding "freedom of belief". The Vatican reassured Vietnamese authorities that the Church did not intend to engage in any political activities.

April 2009: State media launched a new campaign against the two Redemptorists it accused of trying to overthrow the regime, which is a capital offence. The two clergy had joined a campaign opposing the development of bauxite deposits in the highlands of central Vietnam. Reports indicated that extraction of such deposits would cause irrevocable damage to the environment and prove harmful to local residents.

June 2009: In Long Xuyen, capital of An Gang province, southern Vietnam, bulldozers demolished the Convent of the Brothers of the Sacred Family of Banam. The authorities provided no explanation for their actions.

June 2009: In Thu Thiem, a suburb in Ho Chi Minh City, district authorities summoned the Sisters of the Congregation of the Lovers of Holy Cross and told them to leave their site where they had been for 170 years. The building stands on a 3.5 hectare plot also containing a church, a school, a farm, a care facility, a clinic and a kindergarten for about 400 children.

June 2009: The authorities rejected a request by parishioners that Fr Peter Nguyen Van Phuong, a Dominican friar working in Dak Lak province, in the Central Highlands, be allowed to continue his pastoral work in the area. The People's Committee of Lak County stated: "No religious establishment has been present in those areas; therefore, there is no need for religion. The faithful in those four villages can practise their religion at home."

September 2009: Police clashed with parishioners after they interrupted a catechism class at the parish of Loan Ly, in Loc Hai, Phu Loc District.

October 2009: Hundreds of police officers attacked the faithful and fenced off Loan Ly School, which was confiscated from the Archdiocese of Hue.

October 2009: Authorities in Son La allowed a Mass to go ahead but only with police in attendance. The security officials took pictures of more than 500 faithful present at the service. Authorities had previously expelled priests entering Son La, saying they were "not needed" as "there are no Christians" in the province. However, diocesan statistics suggested that at least 3,000 Catholics were living there. However, since 2004 they have been forced to meet secretly.

November 2009: Police detained Fr Peter Nguyen Van Huu, parish priest of Bau Sen, as he was on his way to the bishop's residence in Xa Doai. During his detention, dozens of police officers in anti-riot gear, escorted by militants, removed the statue of Our Lady from the parish cemetery.

November 2009: Authorities in Da Lat, southern Vietnam, began tearing down the Saint Pius X Pontifical Institute to build a "cultural and urban park".

December 2009: Vietnamese President Nguyên Minh Triêt met Benedict XVI at the Vatican. Their talk was reported as being "cordial" but unusually long. In its press release the Holy See "expressed the hope that outstanding questions may be resolved as soon as possible". This was seen as a reference to concerns about religious freedom, which is still limited in the country.[351]

January 2010: Police in Phu Yen Province summoned 55-year-old Pastor Ksor Y Du for questioning. On his way to the police station, security officials stopped Pastor Du and chained him to his motorbike. Reports say Pastor Du was forced to run behind the bike. Falling over several times he was dragged along the ground. He was then beaten and forced to keep running. Du was then carried to the station and was put in Phu Lam prison. No formal charges were brought against him until October. Reports suggest Pastor Du was regularly beaten while in prison. In November Pastor Du was sentenced to six years, with four years house arrest, for "undermining national unity". [352]

March 2010: 63-year-old human rights activist Fr Nguyen Van Ly was released from prison in order to receive medical treatment. He suffered three strokes while in jail leaving the right side of his body partially paralysed. He was also suffering from a brain tumour. Fr Ly said: "They [the Vietnamese government] didn't want to be responsible for the treatment of my tumour, which is complicated, and they wanted to improve their standing in the international community." He was serving an eight-year prison sentence for disseminating anti-government propaganda. Although released from jail, he was placed under house arrest. [353]

April 2010: Christian convert Sung Cua Po was forced to flee into the forest with his family following a series of threats and attacks. Po, who converted in November 2009, received 70 blows to his head and back from local officials and police. Following an altercation with his father over offerings to family ancestors, Nam Son district police were authorised by Dien Bien Dong district authorities to demolish Po's house if deemed necessary. Later, community members confiscated 40 sacks of rice, the family's supply for the year, and stole all their cooking and eating utensils. Eventually local authorities and villagers finally tore down the family's house. Five days later he fled with his wife and three children. [354]

May 2010: K'pa Lot, a Christian, was arrested for "publicly expressing his Christian faith" and was imprisoned in Phu Yen province. Mr Lot was later taken to hospital with bruises on his face and body. He told his wife he had been regularly tortured in prison and beaten daily. [355]

May 2010: During the funeral procession of 82-year-old Mary Tan, police intervened to prevent her burial in the local cemetery. For almost an hour there were clashes between 500 faithful and riot police, who wounded many Catholics and arrested 59 people. Six parishioners from Con Dau were reported to provincial authorities in Da Nang for "disturbing public order" and "attacking state security personnel who were performing their lawful duty". The coffin was taken from the woman's family and cremated. The government has had a long-standing plan to build an "eco-city" on the land. For the project to go ahead, 400 families would have had to leave and a cemetery resited.[356]

June 2010: The Vatican and Vietnam agreed to the papal appointment of a "non-resident representative to the Holy See from Vietnam". Vatican spokesman Fr Federico Lombardi called it "a very significant step" towards better relations. Fr Lombardi explained that the new position did not establish full diplomatic relations between the two sides. He made clear that the representative was not an Apostolic Nuncio or a permanent delegate to Vietnam.[357]

July 2010: In a letter addressed "to any government office within the law of the Socialist Republic of Vietnam, journalists and public figures", Sister Patrick de la Croix Huynh Thi Bich Ngoc, Mother Superior of the Sisters of St Paul of Chartres, asked the local authorities to apologise for the false accusations made against her congregation. She demanded US$6,376,400 compensation for the confiscation of a property "belonging to the diocese of Vinh Long dating back to 1871 and built by generations of nuns". The building was seized on 7th September 1977 for use as a "children's hospital and provincial hospital". No hospital was ever established. Local authorities accused the Sisters of having used the orphanage to "train young dropouts to create forces that oppose the Revolution and the liberation of the Vietnamese people" – a charge that can carry the death penalty. In 2008 the local government authorised the Saigon-Vinh Long Travel Agency to build a four-star luxury hotel on the site but, following fierce protests from the Sisters, the People's Committee decided to build a public square with gardens instead.[358]

Yemen

Population	Religions	Christian Population
24 million	Muslim 99% Other (including Christian) 1%	8,000

Reports point to increasing radicalisation within Yemeni society, a phenomenon witnessed by the thousands of women who protested against setting a minimum age for marriage – 17 for women, 18 for men. Marching through the streets in March 2010 dressed in black niqabs, they defended the Arab Muslim tradition of 'child brides' as young as eight and held up placards which read: "Do not prohibit what God has made possible."[359]

The constitution declares Islam to be the state religion and that *Shari'a* law is the source of all legislation. Christians are able to worship with relative freedom in the few places of worship designated to them. There are reportedly four churches in Aden: three Catholic and one Anglican.[360]

For Yemen's few and isolated Christian faithful, the problem of living in a strictly Islamic milieu has become much worse with the prominence of Al Qaeda, whose growing influence comes at a time of reports pointing to the waning power of Yemen's central government. The January 2009 merger between two regional offshoots of the Islamist network to form Al Qaeda in the Arab Peninsula was the precursor to violence aimed at purging Yemen of non-Islamic influences. More recently, AQIP have claimed responsibility for international terrorism including the October 2010 bomb intercepted in the UK on an aeroplane from Yemen bound for the USA.

Meanwhile disturbing reports coming out of Yemen indicate worsening conditions for many of the country's Christian faithful, who largely come from abroad, particularly Ethiopia. There are increasing concerns about Christians suffering harassment and violence for refusing to abandon their faith. This coincides with an upsurge in attacks on the country's rapidly decreasing Jewish community, the only indigenous non-Muslim religious minority. Two functioning synagogues in the Amran Governorate were closed following anti-Jewish violence in the winter of 2008-09.[361]

July 2009: A report was issued highlighting the plight of Ethiopian Christian immigrants living under extremely difficult social, cultural and economic conditions in Yemen. The report cited evidence of the authorities in the capital, Sana'a, refusing to give permission for Christians to be buried. In order for the burial to go ahead, the name of the deceased had to be changed to a recognised Muslim name. The Yemeni authorities only accepted the name change as genuine if the process was verified by an Muslim authorised to do so. The change in name involved a fee, presumably payable by the deceased's relatives.[362]

June 2009: Two German Bible School students and a Korean were shot dead in Yemen. 24-year-old Anita Gruenwald and 26-year-old Rita Stumpp were studying at an Evangelical Bible School in Lemgo, western Germany and were members of a Baptist Church in Wolfsburg, north Germany. The two were on a short-term internship at the Al Jumhuri Hospital in Saada, north Yemen, and were part of a group of nine people who were kidnapped on a day trip outside the capital. Among the group was Young-Sun I, a 34-year-old Korean woman who was also killed. The nurses were later implicated in Christian missionary activity in Yemen. According to a (UK) *Sunday Times* report, published in July 2009, a German team investigating the crime had evidence that the nurses had been warned to stop converting Muslims. Mullahs had reportedly spoken out against their missionary activities and their books on Christianity had been confiscated. The group included a British engineer only known as Anthony, and a young German couple, Johannes and Sabine Hentshel and their three children: Lydia, four; Anna, three; and 11-month-old Simon. In May 2010 the two girls were rescued in an operation close to the Yemeni-Saudi border involving the governments of both countries. The whereabouts of the rest of the family and Anthony was still unknown.[363]

February 2010: The Yemen-based wing of Al Qaeda called on Muslims in the Arabian Peninsula to wage *jihad* (holy war) against Christians and Jews in the area. Yemen Al Qaeda deputy leader Saeed al Shehri, a former inmate at the US prison in Guantanamo Bay, said in an audio recording posted on an Islamist website: "You have no option out of this plight other than to wage *jihad* [against Christians and Jews]. We advise you, our people in the Peninsula, to prepare and carry your weapons and to defend our religion and yourselves..."[364]

Notes

Where not otherwise stated information is taken from ACN's *Religious Freedom in the World* report 2010 and other ACN sources.

[1] Catholic Hierarchy (www.catholic-hierarchy.org).

[2] International Christian Concern (ICC), *Hall of Shame 2011* (http://www.persecution.org/pdf/2011HallofShame.pdf).

[3] Ibid.

[4] *Catholic Herald*, 24/12/10.

[5] Open Doors,13/02/09.

[6] AsiaNews, 15/06/10.

[7] BosNewsLife, 25/6/10; Christian Solidarity Worldwide (CSW), June 2010; AsiaNews, 15/10/10.

[8] UK Parliament Early Day Motion, 06/07/10.

[9] *The Washington Post*, 09/08/10.

[10] The following figures are based on ACN's 2010 *Religious Freedom in the World* Report, the *CIA World Fact Book* (2010), and other sources from the countries concerned. Please note all figures are approximate.

[11] Afrol News, 03/07/09.

[12] BBC News (web), 05/10/10; ASSIST News Service (ANS), 06/10/10.

[13] Compass Direct News (CDN), 23/04/2010.

[14] CDN, 01/06/10.

[15] CDN, 23/04/10.

[16] CDN, 02/11/10.

[17] CDN, 27/12/10.

[18] Forum 18, 11/06/09.

[19] Forum 18, 11/11/09.

[20] Forum 18, 25/08/09.

[21] *The Tablet*, 17/04/10.

[22] Zenit, 20/08/10.

[23] Forum 18, 07/01/09.

[24] Forum 18, 26/01/09.

[25] Ibid.

[26] Forum 18, 11/02/09.

[27] Forum 18, 30/03/09.

[28] Forum 18, 05/01/10.

[29] Forum 18, 30/07/10.

[30] Zenit, 20/08/10.

[31] Zenit, 08/12/10.

[32] US State Department (Bureau of Democracy, Human Rights, and Labor), *International Religious Freedom Report 2010*: Bosnia and Herzegovina (17/11/10).

[33] Ioannis Michaletos, "An outlook of radical Islamism in Bosnia" (http://www.persecution.org/2010/10/10/an-outlook-of-radical-islamism-in-bosnia/).

[34] US State Department, *International Religious Freedom Report 2009:* Bosnia and Herzegovina (26/10/09).

[35] Ibid.

[36] US State Department, *International Religious Freedom Report 2010*: Bosnia and Herzegovina, (17/11/10).

[37] Ibid.

[38] Serbianna, 22/10/10. (http://serbianna.com/news/?p=6399).

[39] Human Rights Watch, *We are like Forgotten People: The Chin People of Burma* (27/01/09); CDN, 20/02/10.

[40] CSW, *Visit to the Thailand-Burma Border* (08/03/10).

[41] ICC, 25/10/10.

[42] BBC Country Profile: China (http://news.bbc.co.uk/1/hi/world/asia-pacific/country _profiles/1287798.stm).

[43] US State Department, *International Religious Freedom Report 2010*: China, (17/11/2010).

[44] Ibid.

[45] *Catholic Herald*, 24/12/10

[46] Zenit, 08/07/10.

[47] ANS, 20/01/09.

[48] CDN 11/02/09 & 09/04/09.

[49] AsiaNews, 17/02/09.

[50] AsiaNews, 30/03/09.

[51] AsiaNews, 31/03/09.

[52] AsiaNews, 03/07/09.

[53] ChinaAid, 20/07/09.

[54] ChinaAid, 23/08/09.

[55] Holy Spirit Study Centre (http://www.hsstudyc.org.hk/en/china/en_cinfo_china_up09.html).

[56] 3 News (web), 11/12/09 (http://www.3news.co.nz/Fast-growing-Christian-churches-crushed-in-China-/tabid/209/articleID/133686/Default.aspx?ArticleID=133686); Reuters, 11/12/09.

[57] ChinaAid, 04/03/10.

[58] *The Tablet*, 17/04/10; AsiaNews, 08/04/2010 & 12/04/2010.

[59] ChinaAid, 12/05/10.

[60] CDN 10/05/10.

[61] Zenit, 08/07/10.

[62] Zenit, 14/07/10.

[63] Communique of the Press office of the Holy See (November 2010); UCAN, 24/11/10.
[64] AsiaNews, 7/12/10.
[65] BBC News (web), 19/04/10.
[66] *Christian Telegraph*, April 2010.
[67] CSW, *Religious Freedom in Cuba* (01/08/10).
[68] Globalpost, 14/10/10.
[69] BBC News (web), 04/11/10.
[70] US State Department, *International Religious Freedom Report 2009: Democratic Republic of the Congo* (03/11/10).
[71] BBC News (web), 19/01/09.
[72] US State Department, *International Religious Freedom Report 2009: Democratic Republic of the Congo* (03/11/10) quoting Human Rights Watch.
[73] ACN News, 08/12/10.
[74] Zenit, 15/11/10.
[75] AsiaNews, 13/03/10.
[76] Zenit, 09/09/10.
[77] AsiaNews, 24/11/10 & 25/11/10.
[78] BBC News, 01/01/11, AsiaNews, 1/1/11 & 3/1/11 (Fr Samir Khalil Samir SJ).
[79] Christian Post, 11/01/11.
[80] Christian Post, 18/02/10.
[81] US Department of State, *International Religious Freedom Report 2009:* Eritrea (26/10/09).
[82] ICC, 23/02/10.

[83] US Department of State, *International Religious FreedomReport 2010:* Eritrea (17/11/10).
[84] MNN, 08/04/09.
[85] CDN, 21/01/09.
[86] MNN, 08/04/09.
[87] In Chains for Christ, 04/06/09.
[88] MNN, 21/10/09.
[89] MNN, 17/09/09.
[90] Ibid.
[91] ICC, 16/12/09.
[92] In Chains for Christ, 11/01/10.
[93] Christian Post, 18/05/10.
[94] In Chains for Christ, 17/03/10.
[95] ANS, 31/03/10.
[96] ICC,13/05/10.
[97] CDN, 27/07/10.
[98] MNN, 04/11/10.
[99] All India Christian Council (http://indian christians.in/news/content/view/2332/45/); AsiaNews, 11/04/2008.
[100] Cf. *Archbishop Raphael Cheenath of Cuttack-Bhubaneswar's Memorandum to Chief Minister Naveen Pattnaik at their Bhubaneswar* (13/09/10).
[101] CDN, 31/ 20/09.
[102] US State Department, *International Religious Freedom Report 2010:* India (17/11/10).
[103] Cf, ibid.]
[104] Ibid.
[105] ACN News, 23/02/09.
[106] ACN News, 24/07/09.
[107] ANS, 10/12/09.
[108] ANS, 15/01/10; CDN, 20/04/10.
[109] AsiaNews, 01/25/10.
[110] CDN, 20/04/10.

[111] CDN, 01/02/10.
[112] CDN, 20/04/10.
[113] Ibid.
[114] Ibid.
[115] CDN, 22/03/10.
[116] Ibid.
[117] AsiaNews, 19/04/10.
[118] Christian Today, 20/04/10.
[119] Zenit, 19/08/10.
[120] Zenit, 19/08/10; Cath News India, 17/08/10 (http://www.cathnewsindia.com/2010/08/17/%E2%80%98weed-out%E2%80%99-christians-remark-sparks-outrage/).
[121] AsiaNews, 14/09/10 & 15/09/10; AP 15/06/10.
[122] Christian Today, 22/08/10.
[123] ICC, 24/11/10.
[124] AsiaNews, 07/12/10.
[125] AsiaNews, 03/11/10.
[126] AsiaNews, 28/10/10.
[127] CDN, 02/02/09.
[128] CDN, 21/01/09.
[129] CDN, 13/10/09.
[130] CDN, 01/12/09.
[131] CDN, 04/02/10.
[132] AsiaNews, 08/02/10.
[133] CDN, 25/02/10.
[134] CDN, 25/03/10.
[135] UCAN, 07/05/10.
[136] CDN, 09/08/10.
[137] UCAN, 17/09/10.
[138] UCAN, 02/11/10.
[139] Cf. CSW briefing, September 2009.
[140] Foreign Policy (web), 02/11/10 (http://www.foreignpolicy.com/articles/2010/11/02/the_end_of_christianity_in_the_middle_east?page=0,1).
[141] CDN, 20/05/09.
[142] Christian Post, 11/07/09.

143 CDN, 06/01/10.
144 CDN, 28/01/10.
145 ANS, 21/02/10; Christian Post, 04/03/10; CDN, 05/04/10.
146 Baptist Press, 29/10/10.
147 APF, 11/11/10.
148 AP, 11/01/11
149 UNCHR quoted by Fides, 03/04/10.
150 Fides, "Iraq – A brief overview" (04/03/10).
151 Ibid.
152 www.catholic-hierarchy.org
153 Ibid.
154 ACN News, 27/04/09.
155 *New York Times*, 12/07/09.
156 ACN News, 28/09/10.
157 SIR news agency, 25/07/10.
158 ACN News, 27/01/10.
159 ACN News, 18/02/10.
160 ACN News, 07/05/10; Zenit, 03/05/10.
161 Radio Free Europe/Radio Liberty, "Iraq admits minorities remain vulnerable", 20/08/10 (.http://www.unhcr.org/refworld/publisher,RFERL,,,4c7633cb1e,0.html)
162 *The Tablet*, 15/11/10; ACN News, 01-15/11/10; Ankawa News, 01-10/11/10).
163 AsiaNews, 29/11/10.
164 Zenit, 06/12/10; AsiaNews 06/12/10
165 AsiaNews, 31/12/10.
166 *First Pastoral Letter of H.B. Msgr. Fouad Twal, Latin Patriarch of Jerusalem, On the Occasion of Pope Benedict XVI's Visit to the Holy Land, 8-15 May 2009*, (http://www.lpj.org/index.php?option=com_content&view=article&id=204%3Apremiere-lettre-pastorale-du-patriarche-fouad&catid=36%3Adiscours&Itemid=67&lang=en).
167 ACN News, 11/08/09.
168 Holy See Press Office, 23/10/10.
169 Reuters, 04/08/09.
170 ACN News, 08/01/09.
171 ACN News, 30/04/09.
172 ACN News, 08/01/09 & 23/01/10.
173 ACN News, 25/05/09.
174 ACN interviews, Holy Land, December 2007.
175 ACN News, 15/05/09.
176 AsiaNews, 13/05/09.
177 New Tang Dynasty TV (http://english.ntdtv.com/ntdtv_en/ns_me/2009-05-26/074413891248.html); ICC, 26/05/29.
178 ANS, 01/08/09.
179 CDN, 28/12/09.
180 *Jerusalem Post*, 24/03/10.
181 Zenit, 18/05/10.
182 CDN, 04/11/10.
183 *Statement by the United Nations Independent Expert on minority issues, Ms. Gay McDougall, on conclusion of her official visit to Viet Nam – 5 to 15 July 2010* (http://www.ohchr.org/EN/NewsEvents/Pages/DisplayNews.aspx?NewsID=10223&LangID=E).
184 Forum 18, 03/02/09.
185 Forum 18, 09/06/09.
186 Forum 18, 10/07/09.
187 Ibid.
188 Forum 18, 27/08/09.
189 Forum 18, 05/11/09.
190 Forum 18, 01/12/09.
191 Forum 18, 23/12/09.
192 Ibid.
193 Forum 18,10/02/10.
194 Forum 18, 01/10/10.
195 Forum 18, 23/06/10.
196 ICC, Laos profile (http://www.persecution.org/suffering/countryinfodetail.php?countrycode=17)
197 CDN, 10/07/2009.
198 ICC, 11/09/09 & 12/11/09.
199 CDN, 08/02/10; *L'Eglise dans le monde*, 149 (June 2010), pp. 20-21.
200 AsiaNews, 04/16/10.
201 CDN, 14/05/10.
202 CDN, 09/11/10.
203 CDN, 06/01/11.
204 *Lebanon Daily Star*, 28/09/09.
205 2010 UNHCR country operations profile: Lebanon.
206 ACN News, 05/11/09.
207 AsiaNews, 02/16/10.
208 AsiaNews, 02/20/10.
209 AsiaNews, 04/23/10.
210 AsiaNews, 03/25/10.
211 BosNews, 25/06/2010.
212 Ibid.
213 Christian Today, 29/07/10.
214 Officially, the country states it is 100 percent Muslim, so it is impossible to accurately calculate the number of Christians.
215 Open Doors, 2010 World Watch List (http://www.opendoorsuk.org/resources/wwl.php?country=06).
216 US State Department, *International Religious*

Freedom Report 2010:
Maldives (17/11/10).
[217]Forum 18, 18/02/09.
[218] R. Upadhay, "Islamic
Radicalisation of
Maldives", South Asia
Analysis Group Paper no.
2610 (07/03/08).
[219] AsiaTimes Online,
11/11/09.
[220] Forum 18, 23/06/09.
[221] AsiaTimes Online,
11/11/09.
[222] Forum 18, 07/12/09.
[223] US State Department,
*International Religious
Freedom Report 2010*:
Maldives (17/11/10).
[224] Open Doors, 2010
World Watch List
(http://www.opendoorsuk.
org/resources/documents/
WorldWatchList.pdf).
[225] Zenit, 16/03/10.
[226] Ibid.
[227] ACN News: 22/01/10.
[228] Most Rev. Ignatius A.
Kaigama, Catholic
Archbishop of Jos,
*Herdsmen (Pastoralists)
raid Villages near Jos,
Plateau State, Nigeria: A
report* (09/03/10).
[229] CDN 21/04/10.
[230] CDN, 21/05/10.
[231] Independent Catholic
News, 11/07/10.
[232] CDN, AsiaNews, *The
Guardian*/AP, 28/12/10.
[233] Open Doors, World
Watch List prayer profile:
North Korea "still the most
difficult place in the world
to be a Christian"
(http://www. Opendoors
uk.org/resources/wwl.php?
country=01).

[234] US State Department,
*International Religious
Freedom Report 2010*:
North Korea (17/11/10).
[235] *Annuario Pontificio*
(the Vatican's Pontifical
Yearbook), 2010.
[236] AsiaNews, 08/05/10.
[237] BBC News (web),
05/12/10.
[238] AsiaNews, 08/05/10;
BBC News (web),
24/07/09.
[239] ANS, 01/08/09.
[240] CSW 04/01/10 &
08/02/10.
[241] US State Department,
*International Religious
Freedom Report 2010*:
North Korea (17/11/10).
[242] ACN News, 27/01/09.
[243] Christian Today
30/04/09.
[244] ACN News, 01/05/09.
[245] Christian Post,
18/05/09.
[246] ACN News, 08/07/09;
WorldNetDaily, 06/03/10.
[247] ACN News, 03/07/09;
UCAN, 31/07/09.
[248] ACN News, 03/08/09.
[249] ACN News, 16/09/09.
[250] Episcopal News
Service, 06/11/09.
[251] CDN, 14/12/09.
[252] CDN, 05/02/10.
[253] ACN News, 28/01/10.
[254] BBC News (web),
10/03/10.
[255] CDN, 22/03/10.
[256] CDN, 28/04/10.
[257] ANS, 08/05/10.
[258] ANS, 06/05/10.
[259] CDN, 14/05/10.
[260] CDN, 27/05/10 &
07/06/10.
[261] CDN, 07/06/10.
[262] CDN, 25/06/10.

[263] Minorities Concern
Pakistan, 23/07/10; CDN,
26/07/10.
[264] BBC News (South
Asia) 20 07 2010.
[265] CDN, 13/0710.
[266]CDN, 21/10/10.
[267] ACN News, 29/11/10.
[268] BBC News, 4/1/11.
[269] ACN News: 10/05/10.
[270] Christian Post,
13/06/10.
[271] AsiaNews, 27/12/10.
[272] Forum 18, 10/09/08.
[273] Forum 18, 26/05/09;
AsiaNews, 05/07/09.
[274] Forum 18, 02/06/09;
AsiaNews, 05/07/09.
[275] Forum 18, 02/03/09.
[276] ACN News, 28/01/09.
[277] Zenit, 19/05/10.
[278] Forum 18, 26/02/09.
[279] Forum 18, 02/10/09.
[280] Forum 18, 23/11/09.
[281] ANS, 15/12/09.
[282] Forum 18, 23/03/10.
[283] Forum 18, 11/06/10.
[284] AsiaNews, 12/11/10;
Interfax News, 15/11/10;
Forum 18, 14/12/10.
[285] Forum 18, 14/12/10.
[286] US State Department,
*International Religious
Freedom Report 2010*:
Saudi Arabia (17/11/10).
[287] Center for Religious
Freedom of the Hudson
Institute, *Saudi Arabia's
Curriculum of Intolerance*,
2008 update.
[288] Open Doors, World
Watch List 2010 (http://
www.opendoorsuk.org/
resources/country-profiles.
php).
[289] US State Department,
International Religious

Freedom Report 2010:
Saudi Arabia (11/03/10).
[290] AsiaNews, 03/10/09.
[291] AsiaNews, 31/12/09.
[292] Bloomberg news,
11/08/10.
[293] AsiaNews, 07/10/10.
[294] Ibid.
[295] ACN News, 11/03/09.
[296] Internal Displacement
Monitoring Centre – UN
OCHA reports October
2010 (www.internal-
displacement.org/idmc/we
bsite/countries.nsf).
[297] CSW, *Sri Lanka:
Religious freedom in the
post-conflict situation*
(2010).
[298] CDN, 17/08/09.
[299] CSW, *Sri Lanka:
Religious freedom in the
post-conflict situation*
(2010).
[300] CDN, 26/01/09.
[301] AsiaNews, 03/21/09.
[302] CDN, 26/01/09.
[303] TamilNet, 26/12/08.
[304] ACN News, 14/01/09.
[305] ACN News, 04/02/09.
[306] ACN News, 11/03/09.
[307] CDN, 16/04/09.
[308] Ibid.
[309] Ibid.
[310] CDN, 17/08/09.
[311] Ibid.
[312] Ibid.
[313] AsiaNews, 06/25/09.
[314] ACN News, 01/05/09.
[315] CDN, 17/08/09.
[316] Ibid.
[317] Ibid.
[318] Ibid.
[319] Ibid.
[320] AsiaNews, 09/12/09.
[321] CSW Weekly
Summary, 18/11/09.
[322] AsiaNews, 17/05/10.

[323] UCAN, 02/07/10.
[324] US State Department,
*International Religious
Freedom Report 2010:*
Sudan (17/11/10).
[325] CDN, 13/4/09.
[326] AFP, 080/9/09; Reuters,
22/10/09.
[327] ACN News, 18/09/09/;
US State Department,
*International Religious
Freedom Report 2010:*
Sudan (17/11/10).
[328] ACN News, 13/10/10.
[329] ACN/SCIAF Press
Release, 03/12/10.
[330] AsiaNews, 10/06/10.
[331] CSW, Turkey Religious
Freedom Profile
(01/09/09), Executive
Summary.
[332] Hurriyet DailyNews
(web), 05/07/10.
[333] Forum 18, 27/11/10.
[334] BBC News (web),
03/6/10, ACN News,
04/6/10; AsiaNews,
06/7/10 and 16/10/10. On
beheading as a ritual
practice see Timothy R.
Furnish, "Beheading in the
Name of Islam", *Middle
East Quarterly* (2005), pp.
51-57.
[335] AsiaNews, 11/4/10.
[336] Private communication
with ACN, Autumn 2009.
[337] CNS quoted in
CatholicReview.org,
18/08/09 (http://www.
catholicreview.org/subpag
es/storyworldnew-new.
aspx?action=6713).
[338] US State Department,
*International Religious
Freedom Report 2010:*
Venezuela (11/03/10).
[339] Reuters, 03/10/10.

[340] CNS, 09/06/09.
[341] CNS quoted in
CatholicReview.org,
18/08/09 (http://www.
catholicreview.org/subpag
es/storyworldnew-new.
aspx?action=6713).
[342] Zenit, 09/07/10.
[343] CNS, 16/07/10.
[344] *The Tablet*, 05/10/10.
[345] BBC News (web),
14/12/10.
[346] Christian Post,
18/08/10.
[347] US State Department,
*International Religious
Freedom Report 2010*:
Vietnam (17/11/10).
[348] AsiaNews, 06/04/09.
[349] US State Department,
*International Religious
Freedom Report 2010*:
Vietnam (17/11/10).
[350] AsiaNews, 10/03/07.
[351] AsiaNews, 12/11/09.
[352] CDN, 01/04/10.
[353] Christian Today,
18/03/10; Zenit, 17/03/10.
[354] CDN, 01/04/10.
[355] Assist News, 01/05/10.
[356] AsiaNews, 19/05/10;
AFP, 05/05/10.
[357] CNA/EWTN, 26/06/10.
[358] AsiaNews, 07/13/10.
[359] AsiaNews, 23/03/10.
[360] US State Department,
*International Religious
Freedom Report 2010*:
Yemen (17/11/10).
[361] Ibid.
[362] Orato, 13/07/09
(www.orato.com/world-
affairs/christians-denied-
funerals-yemen).
[363] Christian Post,
18/05/10; *Sunday Times*,
21/07/09.
[364] Reuters, 08/02/10.

About *Aid to the Church in Need*

Aid to the Church in Need supports Christians wherever they are persecuted, oppressed or in pastoral need. ACN is a Catholic charity, helping to bring Christ to the world.

Founded on Christmas Day 1947 ACN is now a universal pastoral charity of the Catholic Church, with thousands of projects all over the world. Every year the charity responds to more than 5,000 requests for aid from bishops and religious superiors in around 140 countries:

- Seminarians are trained

- Bibles and religious literature are printed

- Priests and religious are supported

- Refugees are helped

- Churches and chapels are built and restored

- Over 48 million of ACN's Child's Bible have been printed, in more than 162 languages

- Religious programmes are broadcast

For regular updates from the suffering Church around the world and to view our full range of books, cards, gifts and music, please log on to ACN's national website in your country (see over).

> *Thank you for helping to dry the tears of the abandoned Jesus on the crosses of this century.*
> Fr Werenfried van Straaten, O. Praem,
> founder of *Aid to the Church in Need*

 **Aid to the Church in Need**

Aid to the Church in Need
United Kingdom

12-14 Benhill Avenue
Sutton
Surrey
SM1 4DA
United Kingdom

Telephone: +44 (0) 20 8642 8668
Email: acn@acnuk.org
Website: www.acnuk.org

Australia

PO Box 6245
Blacktown DC
NSW 2148
Australia

Telephone: +61 (0) 2 9679 1929
Email: info@aidtochurch.org
Website: www.aidtochurch.org

Canada

P.O. Box 670, STN H
Montreal
QC H3G 2M6
Canada

Telephone: +1 514 932 0552
   or +1 800 585 6333
Email: info@acn-aed-ca.org
Website: www.acn-aed-ca.org

Ireland

151 St Mobhi Road
Glasnevin
Dublin 9
Ireland

Telephone: +353 (0) 1 83 77 516
Email: churchinneed@eircom.net
Website: www.acnirl.org

United States of America

725 Leonard Street
PO Box 220384
Brooklyn NY 11222-0384
USA

Telephone: +1 (1) 800 628 6333
Email: info@churchinneed.org
Website: www.churchinneed.org

International Headquarters

ACN International
(Postal Address)

Bischof-Kindermann-Straße 23
D-61462 Königstein/Ts.
Germany

Telephone: +49 (0) 61 74 291 0
Email: info@acn-intl.org
Website: www.acn-intl.org

ACN International
(P.O. Box Address)

Postfach 12 09
D-61452 Königstein/Ts.
Germany